An Anthology of Australian Verse

Edited by Bertram Stevens

Contents

Preface 7
Introduction 8
William Charles Wentworth 17
   Australasia 17
Charles Harpur 19
   Love 19
   Words 19
   A Coast View 20
William Forster 21
   'The Love in her Eyes lay Sleeping' 21
James Lionel Michael 23
   'Through Pleasant Paths' 23
   Personality 24
Daniel Henry Deniehy 26
   Love in a Cottage 26
   A Song for the Night 28
Richard Rowe 30
   Superstites Rosae 30
   Soul Ferry 30
Sir Henry Parkes 32
   The Buried Chief 32
Thomas Alexander Browne ('Rolf Boldrewood') 33
   Perdita 33
Adam Lindsay Gordon 35
   A Dedication 35
   Thora's Song 37
   The Sick Stock-rider 38
Henry Kendall 41
   Prefatory Sonnets 41
   September in Australia 43
   Rose Lorraine 44
   To a Mountain 47
   Araluen 49
   After Many Years 51
   Hy-Brasil 54
   Outre Mer 55
Marcus Clarke 57
   The Song of Tigilau 57
Patrick Moloney 60
   Melbourne 60
Alfred Domett 61
   An Invitation 61
   A Maori Girl's Song 62
James Brunton Stephens 64
   The Dominion of Australia 64
   The Dark Companion 66
Thomas Bracken 70
   Not Understood 70
   Spirit of Song 71
Ada Cambridge 73
   What of the Night? 73
   Good-bye 74
   The Virgin Martyr 75
   Honour 76
   Despair 76
   Faith 77
Alexander Bathgate 78
   The Clematis 78
Philip Joseph Holdsworth 79
   Quis Separabit? 79
   My Queen of Dreams 80
Mary Hannay Foot 81
   Where the Pelican Builds 81
   New Country 82
   No Message 84
   Happy Days 85
Henry Lea Twisleton 86
   To a Cabbage Rose 86

Mrs. James Glenny Wilson 88
   Fairyland 88
   A Winter Daybreak 89
   The Lark's Song 91
Edward Booth Loughran 92
   Dead Leaves 92
   Isolation 93
   Ishmonie 95
John Liddell Kelly 96
   Immortality 96
   Heredity 96
Robert Richardson 97
   A Ballade of Wattle Blossom 97
   A Song 99
James Lister Cuthbertson 100
   Australia Federata 100
   At Cape Schanck 102
   The Australian Sunrise 105
John Farrell 106
   Australia to England 106
Arthur Patchett Martin 111
   Bushland 111
Douglas Brooke Wheelton Sladen 112
   Under the Wattle 112
Victor James Daley 113
   Players 113
   Anna 114
   The Night Ride 116
Alice Werner 118
   Bannerman of the Dandenong 118
Ethel Castilla 120
   An Australian Girl 120
   A Song of Sydney 121
Francis William Lauderdale Adams 123
   Something 123
   Gordon's Grave 124
   To A. L. Gordon 124
   Love and Death 125
Thomas William Heney 126
   A Riverina Road 127
Patrick Edward Quinn 129
   A Girl's Grave 129
John Sandes 131
Inez K. Hyland 133
   To a Wave 133
   Bread and Wine 134
George Essex Evans 135
   An Australian Symphony 135
   A Nocturne 138
   A Pastoral 139
   The Women of the West 141
Mary Colborne-Veel 143
   'What Look hath She?' 143
   Saturday Night 143
   'Resurgam' 145
      (Autumn Song) 145
   Distant Authors 146
John Bernard O'Hara 148
   Happy Creek 148
   A Country Village 149
   Flinders 152
M. A. Sinclair 154
   The Chatelaine 154
Sydney Jephcott 156
   Chaucer 156
   White Paper 156
   Splitting 158
      Evening 160
   Home-woe 161
   A Ballad of the last King of Thule 162
   The icy Boreal Light 163
   A Fragment 163
Andrew Barton Paterson ('Banjo') 164
   The Daylight is Dying 164
   Clancy of the Overflow 166
   Black Swans 168

The Travelling Post Office	170
The Old Australian Ways	171
By the Grey Gulf-Water	174
Jessie Mackay.	176
The Grey Company	176
A Folk Song	178
Dunedin in the Gloaming	179
The Burial of Sir John Mackenzie	181
(1901)	181
Henry Lawson.	183
Andy's gone with Cattle	183
Out Back	184
The Star of Australasia	186
The Vagabond	190
The Sliprails and the Spur	194
Arthur Albert Dawson Bayldon.	196
Sunset	196
The Sea	196
To Poesy	197
Jennings Carmichael.	198
An Old Bush Road	198
A Woman's Mood	201
Agnes L. Storrie.	203
Twenty Gallons of Sleep	203
A Confession	204
Martha M. Simpson.	205
To an Old Grammar	205
William Gay.	208
Primroses	208
To M.	209
Vestigia Nulla Retrorsum	210
Edward Dyson.	211
The Old Whim Horse	211
Dowell O'Reilly.	214
The Sea-Maiden	214
David MacDonald Ross.	215
Love's Treasure House	215
The Sea to the Shell	216
The Silent Tide	217
The Watch on Deck	218
Autumn	219
Mary Gilmore.	220
A Little Ghost	220
Good-Night	221
Bernard O'Dowd.	222
Love's Substitute	222
Our Duty	223
Edwin James Brady.	224
The Wardens of the Seas	224
Will. H. Ogilvie.	227
Queensland Opal	227
Wind o' the Autumn	228
Daffodils	228
A Queen of Yore	229
Drought	230
The Shadow on the Blind	232
Roderic Quinn.	233
The House of the Commonwealth	233
The Lotus-Flower	236
David McKee Wright.	238
An Old Colonist's Reverie	238
Christopher John Brennan.	240
Romance	240
Poppies	241
John Le Gay Brereton.	242
The Sea Maid	242
Home	243
Wilfred	244
Arthur H. Adams.	246
Bayswater, W.	246
Bond Street	249
Ethel Turner.	250
A Trembling Star	250
'Oh, if that Rainbow up there!'	252
Johannes Carl Andersen.	254

Soft, Low and Sweet	254
Maui Victor	255
Dora Wilcox	257
In London	257
Ernest Currie	260
Laudabunt Alii	260
George Charles Whitney	262
Sunset	262
Ode to Apollo	263
Notes on the Poems	266
Biographical Notes	271

AN ANTHOLOGY OF AUSTRALIAN VERSE

BY

Edited by Bertram Stevens

An Anthology of Australian Verse
Edited by Bertram Stevens

Dedicated to
DAVID SCOTT MITCHELL, Esq.
Sydney

Preface

The Editor has endeavoured to make this selection representative
of the best short poems written by Australians or inspired by
Australian scenery and conditions of life, -- "Australian" in this connection
being used to include New Zealand. The arrangement is
as nearly as possible chronological; and the appendix contains
brief biographical particulars of the authors, together with notes
which may be useful to readers outside Australia.

The Editor thanks Messrs. H. H. Champion, Henry Gyles Turner,

E. B. Loughran, A. Brazier and Walter Murdoch (Melbourne),
Mr. Sydney Jephcott (Upper Murray, Vic.), Mr. Fred. Johns (Adelaide),
Mr. Thomas Cottle (Auckland), Mr. J. C. Andersen (Christchurch),
Messrs. David Scott Mitchell, Alfred Lee, A. W. Jose,
and J. Le Gay Brereton (Sydney), for their generous help.
Mr. Douglas Sladen's anthologies, Messrs. Turner and Sutherland's
"Development of Australian Literature", and `The Bulletin' have also furnished
much useful information.

Introduction

As the literature of a country is, in certain respects,
a reflex of its character, it may be advisable to introduce this Anthology
with some account of the main circumstances which have affected
the production of Australian poetry.

Australia was first settled by the British a little more than a century ago,
so that we are still a young community. The present population,
including that of New Zealand, is a little under five millions,
or about the same as that of London; it is chiefly scattered
along the coast and the few permanent waterways, and a vast central region
is but sparsely inhabited as yet. All climates, from tropical to frigid,
are included within the continent, but the want of satisfactory watersheds
renders it peculiarly liable to long droughts and sudden floods.
The absence of those broad, outward signs of the changing seasons
which mark the pageant of the year in the old world is probably
a greater disadvantage than we are apt to suspect. Here, too,
have existed hardly any of the conditions which obtained in older communities

where great literature arose. There is no glamour of old Romance
about our early history, no shading off from the actual
into a dim region of myth and fable; our beginnings are clearly defined
and of an eminently prosaic character. The early settlers were engaged
in a hand-to-hand struggle with nature, and in the establishment
of the primitive industries. Their strenuous pioneering days
were followed by the feverish excitement of the gold period and a consequent
rapid expansion of all industries. Business and politics have afforded
ready roads to success, and have absorbed the energies of the best intellects.
There has been no leisured class of cultured people to provide the atmosphere
in which literature is best developed as an art; and, until recently,
we have been content to look to the mother country for our artistic standards
and supplies. The principal literary productions of our first century
came from writers who had been born elsewhere, and naturally brought with them
the traditions and sentiments of their home country.

We have not yet had time to settle down and form any decided
racial characteristics; nor has any great crisis occurred
to fuse our common sympathies and create a national sentiment.
Australia has produced no great poet, nor has any remarkable innovation
in verse forms been successfully attempted. But the old forms
have been so coloured by the strange conditions of a new country,
and so charged with the thoughts and feelings of a vigorous,
restless democracy now just out of its adolescence, that they have
an interest and a value beyond that of perhaps technically better minor poetry
produced under English skies.

The first verses actually written and published in Australia seem to have been
the Royal Birthday Odes of Michael Robinson, which were printed as broadsides
from 1810 to 1821. Their publication in book form was announced
in 'The Hobart Town Gazette' of 23rd March, 1822, but no copy of such a vol-

ume is at present known to exist. The famous "Prologue", said to have been recited at the first dramatic performance in Australia, on January 16th, 1796 (when Dr. Young's tragedy "The Revenge" and "The Hotel" were played in a temporary theatre at Sydney), was for a long time attributed to the notorious George Barrington, and ranked as the first verse produced in Australia. There is, however, no evidence to support this claim. The lines first appeared in a volume called "Original Poems and Translations" chiefly by Susannah Watts, published in London in 1802, a few months before the appearance of the "History of New South Wales" (1803) -- known as George Barrington's -- which also, in all probability, was not written by Barrington. In Susannah Watts' book the Prologue is stated to be written by "A Gentleman", but there is no clue to the name of the author. Mr. Barron Field, Judge of the Supreme Court of New South Wales, printed in Sydney in 1819 his "First Fruits of Australian Poetry", for private circulation. Field was a friend of Charles Lamb, who addressed to him the letter printed in "The Essays of Elia" under the title of "Distant Correspondents". Lamb reviewed the "First Fruits" in `The Examiner', and one wishes for his sake that the verses were more worthy.

The first poem of any importance by an Australian is William Charles Wentworth's "Australasia", written in 1823 at Cambridge University in competition for the Chancellor's medal. There were twenty-seven competitors, and the prize was awarded to W. Mackworth Praed, Wentworth being second on the list. Wentworth's poem was printed in London in the same year, and shortly afterwards in `The Sydney Gazette', the first Australian newspaper. In 1826 there was printed at the Albion Press, Sydney, "Wild Notes from the Lyre of a Native Minstrel" by Charles Tompson, Junior, the first verse of an Australian-born writer published in this country.

There was also published in Sydney in 1826 a book of verses
by Dr. John Dunmore Lang, called "Aurora Australis".
Both Lang and Wentworth afterwards conducted newspapers
and wrote histories of New South Wales, but their names are more famous
in the political than in the literary annals of the country.
At Hobart Town in 1827 appeared "The Van Diemen's Land Warriors,
or the Heroes of Cornwall" by "Pindar Juvenal", the first book of verse
published in Tasmania. During the next ten years various poetical effusions
were printed in the colonies, which are of bibliographical interest
but of hardly any intrinsic value. Newspapers had been established
at an early date, but until the end of this period they were little better
than news-sheets or official gazettes, giving no opportunities
for literature. The proportion of well-educated persons was small,
the majority of the free settlers being members of the working classes,
as very few representatives of British culture came willingly to this country
until after the discovery of gold.

It was not until 1845 that the first genuine, though crude,
Australian poetry appeared, in the form of a small volume of sonnets
by Charles Harpur, who was born at Windsor, N.S.W., in 1817.
He passed his best years in the lonely bush, and wrote largely
under the influence of Wordsworth and Shelley. He had some
imagination and poetic faculty of the contemplative order,
but the disadvantages of his life were many. Harpur's best work
is in his longer poems, from which extracts cannot conveniently be given here.
The year 1842 had seen the publication of Henry Parkes' "Stolen Moments",
the first of a number of volumes of verse which that statesman bravely issued,
the last being published just before his eightieth year. The career of Parkes
is coincident with a long and important period of our history,
in which he is the most striking figure. Not the least interesting
aspect of his character, which contained much of rugged greatness,
was his love of poetry and his unfailing kindness to the struggling writers
of the colony. Others who deserve remembrance for their services at this time

are Nicol D. Stenhouse and Dr. Woolley. Among the writers of the period D. H. Deniehy, Henry Halloran, J. Sheridan Moore and Richard Rowe contributed fairly good verse to the newspapers, the principal of which were `The Atlas' (1845-9), `The Empire' (1850-8), and two papers still in existence -- `The Freeman's Journal' (1850) and `The Sydney Morning Herald', which began as `The Sydney Herald' in 1831. None of their writings, however, reflected to any appreciable extent the scenery or life of the new country.

With the discovery of gold a new era began for Australia. That event induced the flow of a large stream of immigration, and gave an enormous impetus to the development of the colonies. Among the ardent spirits attracted here were J. Lionel Michael, Robert Sealy, R. H. Horne, the Howitts, Henry Kingsley and Adam Lindsay Gordon. Michael was a friend of Millais, and an early champion of the Pre-Raphaelite Brotherhood. Soon after his arrival in Sydney he abandoned the idea of digging for gold, and began to practise again as a solicitor. Later on he removed to Grafton on the Clarence River; there in 1857 Henry Kendall, a boy of 16, found work in his office, and Michael, discerning his promise, encouraged him to write. Most of the boy's earliest verses were sent from Michael's office to Parkes, who printed them in his paper `The Empire'. When Kendall left Grafton, Michael gave him a letter of introduction to Stenhouse, which brought him in touch with the small literary group in Sydney; and his first volume, "Poems and Songs", was published in Sydney in 1862. It was not long before he recognised the extreme weakness of most of its contents, and did what he could to suppress the book. He sent specimens of his best work to the London `Athenaeum', and wrote a pathetic letter to the Editor, which was printed in the issue of 27th September, 1862, together with some of the poems and a most kindly comment. Kendall soon wrote again, sending more poems, and received encouraging notices in `The Athenaeum' on 19th September, 1863,

27th February, 1864, and 17th February, 1866. These form
the first favourable pronouncement upon Australian poetry
by an English critical journal of importance. Their stimulating effect
upon Kendall was very great. From the indifference of the many
and the carping criticisms of some of the magnates here,
he had appealed to one of the highest literary authorities in England,
and received praise beyond his wildest expectations.

Meanwhile the colony of Victoria, which began its independent career in 1851,
had been advancing even more rapidly than New South Wales.
`The Argus' newspaper had been in existence since 1846, and other periodicals
sprang up in Melbourne which gave further scope to letters.
`The Australasian' was established in 1854, and soon became
the most important literary journal in Australia. Adam Lindsay Gordon,
who had landed in Adelaide in the same year as Henry Kingsley -- 1853 --
published a little book of verse in 1864 at Mt. Gambier, S.A.,
and began to contribute verses to a Melbourne sporting paper in 1866.
These were printed anonymously, and attracted some attention;
but a collection of his ballads -- "Sea Spray and Smoke Drift" --
brought very little praise and no profit. Marcus Clarke came to Melbourne
in 1864, and soon afterwards began to write for `The Argus' and other papers.
About the same time the presence of R. H. Horne, the distinguished author
of "Orion", in Melbourne lent a lustre to that city,
which was for the time the literary centre of Australia.
Horne corresponded with Kendall, and contributed to a paper
edited by Deniehy in Sydney -- `The Southern Cross' (1859-60).
He was the presiding genius of the literary gatherings
at Dwight's book-shop in Melbourne, and no doubt exercised
a beneficial influence upon the writers around him.

In 1870, after a series of crushing disappointments, Gordon committed suicide.
His dramatic end awakened sympathy and gave an additional interest
to his writings. It was soon found that in the city and the bush

many of his spirited racing ballads were well known. The virile,
athletic tone of his verse, which taught

> "How a man should uphold the sports of his land
> And strike his best with a strong right hand
>   And take his strokes in return" --

and the practical philosophy, summed up in the well-known quatrain --

> "Life is mostly froth and bubble,
>   Two things stand like stone;
> Kindness in another's trouble,
>   Courage in your own" --

appeal strongly to Australians. Gordon's work cannot be considered
as peculiarly Australian in character; but much of it is concerned
with the horse, and all of it is a-throb with the manly, reckless personality
of the writer. Horses and horse-racing are especially interesting
to Australians, the Swinburnian rush of Gordon's ballads charms their ear,
and in many respects he embodies their ideal of a man.
There are few Australians who do not know some of his poems,
even if they know no others, and his influence upon subsequent writers
has been very great.

Brunton Stephens, who came to Queensland in 1866, wrote there a long poem
called "Convict Once" which, when published in London in 1871,
gained high praise from competent critics, and gave the author
an academic reputation. A little book of humorous verses
issued in Melbourne in 1873 almost immediately became popular,
and a later volume of "Miscellaneous Poems" (1880), containing some
fine patriotic utterances as well as many in lighter vein,
established him as one of our chief singers.

The first important poem from New Zealand -- Domett's "Ranolf and Amohia" --
was published in London in 1872. Domett spent thirty years in New Zealand.
He wrote a good deal of verse before leaving England and after his return,
but "Ranolf and Amohia" is the only poem showing traces
of Australian influence. It is a miscellany in verse rather than an epic,
and contains some fine descriptions of New Zealand scenery.

The death of Kendall in Sydney in 1882 closed what may be regarded
as the second literary period. He had published his finest work
in "Songs from the Mountains" (1880), and had the satisfaction of knowing
that it was a success, financially and otherwise. Kendall's audience
is not so large as Gordon's, but it is a steadily growing one;
and many readers who have been affected by his musical verse
hold the ill-fated singer in more tender regard than any other.
He lived at a time when Australians had not learned to think it possible
that any good thing in art could come out of Australia,
and were too fully occupied with things of the market-place
to concern themselves much about literature.

Several attempts have been made to maintain magazines and reviews
in Sydney and Melbourne, but none of them could compete successfully
with the imported English periodicals. `The Colonial Monthly',
`The Melbourne Review', `The Sydney Quarterly', and `The Centennial Magazine'
were the most important of these. They cost more to produce
than their English models, and the fact that their contents were Australian
was not sufficient in itself to obtain for them adequate support.
Newspapers have played a far more important part in our literary world.
`The Australasian', `Sydney Mail' and `Queenslander' have done a good deal
to encourage local writers, but the most powerful influence
has been that of `The Bulletin', started in Sydney in 1880.
Its racy, irreverent tone and its humour are characteristically Australian,

and through its columns the first realistic Australian verse of any importance
-- the writings of Henry Lawson and A. B. Paterson -- became widely known.
When published in book form, their verses met with phenomenal success;
Paterson's "The Man from Snowy River" (1895) having already attained
a circulation of over thirty thousand copies. It is the first
of a long series of volumes, issued during the last ten years, whose character
is far more distinctively Australian than that of their predecessors.
Their number and success are evidences of the lively interest taken
by the present generation here in its native literature.

Australia has now come of age, and is becoming conscious
of its strength and its possibilities. Its writers to-day are, as a rule,
self-reliant and hopeful. They have faith in their own country;
they write of it as they see it, and of their work and their joys and fears,
in simple, direct language. It may be that none of it is poetry
in the grand manner, and that some of it is lacking in technical finish;
but it is a vivid and faithful portrayal of Australia, and its ruggedness
is in character. It is hoped that this selection from the verse that has been
written up to the present time will be found a not unworthy contribution
to the great literature of the English-speaking peoples.

William Charles Wentworth.

Australasia

Celestial poesy! whose genial sway
Earth's furthest habitable shores obey;
Whose inspirations shed their sacred light,
Far as the regions of the Arctic night,
And to the Laplander his Boreal gleam
Endear not less than Phoebus' brighter beam, --
Descend thou also on my native land,
And on some mountain-summit take thy stand;
Thence issuing soon a purer font be seen
Than charmed Castalia or famed Hippocrene;
And there a richer, nobler fane arise,
Than on Parnassus met the adoring eyes.
And tho', bright goddess, on the far blue hills,
That pour their thousand swift pellucid rills
Where Warragamba's rage has rent in twain
Opposing mountains, thundering to the plain,
No child of song has yet invoked thy aid
'Neath their primeval solitary shade, --
Still, gracious Pow'r, some kindling soul inspire,
To wake to life my country's unknown lyre,
That from creation's date has slumbering lain,

Or only breathed some savage uncouth strain;
And grant that yet an Austral Milton's song
Pactolus-like flow deep and rich along, --
An Austral Shakespeare rise, whose living page
To nature true may charm in ev'ry age; --
And that an Austral Pindar daring soar,
Where not the Theban eagle reach'd before.
And, O Britannia! shouldst thou cease to ride
Despotic Empress of old Ocean's tide; --
Should thy tamed Lion -- spent his former might, --
No longer roar the terror of the fight; --
Should e'er arrive that dark disastrous hour,
When bow'd by luxury, thou yield'st to pow'r; --
When thou, no longer freest of the free,
To some proud victor bend'st the vanquish'd knee; --
May all thy glories in another sphere
Relume, and shine more brightly still than here;
May this, thy last-born infant, then arise,
To glad thy heart and greet thy parent eyes;
And Australasia float, with flag unfurl'd,
A new Britannia in another world.

Charles Harpur.

Love

She loves me! From her own bliss-breathing lips
 The live confession came, like rich perfume
 From crimson petals bursting into bloom!
And still my heart at the remembrance skips
Like a young lion, and my tongue, too, trips
 As drunk with joy! while every object seen
 In life's diurnal round wears in its mien
A clear assurance that no doubts eclipse.
And if the common things of nature now
 Are like old faces flushed with new delight,
Much more the consciousness of that rich vow
 Deepens the beauteous, and refines the bright,
 While throned I seem on love's divinest height
'Mid all the glories glowing round its brow.

Words

Words are deeds. The words we hear
May revolutionize or rear
A mighty state. The words we read
May be a spiritual deed

Excelling any fleshly one,
As much as the celestial sun
Transcends a bonfire, made to throw
A light upon some raree-show.
A simple proverb tagged with rhyme
May colour half the course of time;
The pregnant saying of a sage
May influence every coming age;
A song in its effects may be
More glorious than Thermopylae,
And many a lay that schoolboys scan
A nobler feat than Inkerman.

A Coast View

High 'mid the shelves of a grey cliff, that yet
Riseth in Babylonian mass above,
In a benched cleft, as in the mouldered chair
Of grey-beard Time himself, I sit alone,
And gaze with a keen wondering happiness
Out o'er the sea. Unto the circling bend
That verges Heaven, a vast luminous plain
It stretches, changeful as a lover's dream --
Into great spaces mapped by light and shade
In constant interchange -- either 'neath clouds
The billows darken, or they shimmer bright
In sunny scopes of measureless expanse.
'Tis Ocean dreamless of a stormy hour,
Calm, or but gently heaving; -- yet, O God!
What a blind fate-like mightiness lies coiled

In slumber, under that wide-shining face!
While o'er the watery gleam -- there where its edge
Banks the dim vacancy, the topmost sails
Of some tall ship, whose hull is yet unseen,
Hang as if clinging to a cloud that still
Comes rising with them from the void beyond,
Like to a heavenly net, drawn from the deep
And carried upward by ethereal hands.

William Forster.

`The Love in her Eyes lay Sleeping'

  The love in her eyes lay sleeping,
  As stars that unconscious shine,
  Till, under the pink lids peeping,
  I wakened it up with mine;
And we pledged our troth to a brimming oath
  In a bumper of blood-red wine.
  Alas! too well I know
  That it happened long ago;
  Those memories yet remain,
  And sting, like throbs of pain,
  And I'm alone below,
But still the red wine warms, and the rosy goblets glow;

If love be the heart's enslaver,
'Tis wine that subdues the head.
But which has the fairest flavour,
And whose is the soonest shed?
Wine waxes in power in that desolate hour
When the glory of love is dead.
Love lives on beauty's ray,
But night comes after day,
And when the exhausted sun
His high career has run,
The stars behind him stay,
And then the light that lasts consoles our darkening way.
When beauty and love are over,
And passion has spent its rage,
And the spectres of memory hover,
And glare on life's lonely stage,
'Tis wine that remains to kindle the veins
And strengthen the steps of age.
Love takes the taint of years,
And beauty disappears,
But wine in worth matures
The longer it endures,
And more divinely cheers,
And ripens with the suns and mellows with the spheres.

James Lionel Michael.

`Through Pleasant Paths'

Through pleasant paths, through dainty ways,
   Love leads my feet;
Where beauty shines with living rays,
   Soft, gentle, sweet;
The placid heart at random strays,
And sings, and smiles, and laughs and plays,
And gathers from the summer days
   Their light and heat,
That in its chambers burn and blaze
   And beam and beat.

I throw myself among the ferns
   Under the shade,
And watch the summer sun that burns
   On dell and glade;
To thee, my dear, my fancy turns,
In thee its Paradise discerns,
For thee it sighs, for thee it yearns,
   My chosen maid;
And that still depth of passion learns
   Which cannot fade.

The wind that whispers in the night,
  Subtle and free,
The gorgeous noonday's blinding light,
  On hill and tree,
All lovely things that meet my sight,
All shifting lovelinesses bright,
Speak to my heart with calm delight,
  Seeming to be
Cloth'd with enchantment, robed in white,
  To sing of thee.

The ways of life are hard and cold
  To one alone;
Bitter the strife for place and gold --
  We weep and groan:
But when love warms the heart grows bold;
And when our arms the prize enfold,
Dearest! the heart can hardly hold
  The bliss unknown,
Unspoken, never to be told --
  My own, my own!

Personality

"Death is to us change, not consummation."
      Heart of Midlothian.

A change! no, surely, not a change,
  The change must be before we die;
Death may confer a wider range,

From pole to pole, from sea to sky,
It cannot make me new or strange
 To mine own Personality!

For what am I? -- this mortal flesh,
 These shrinking nerves, this feeble frame,
For ever racked with ailments fresh
 And scarce from day to day the same --
A fly within the spider's mesh,
 A moth that plays around the flame!

THIS is not I -- within such coil
 The immortal spirit rests awhile:
When this shall lie beneath the soil,
 Which its mere mortal parts defile,
THAT shall for ever live and foil
 Mortality, and pain, and guile.

Whatever Time may make of me
 Eternity must see me still
Clear from the dross of earth, and free
 From every stain of every ill;
Yet still, where-e'er -- what-e'er I be,
 Time's work Eternity must fill.

When all the worlds have ceased to roll,
 When the long light has ceased to quiver
When we have reached our final goal
 And stand beside the Living River,
This vital spark -- this loving soul,
 Must last for ever and for ever.

To choose what I must be is mine,

Mine in these few and fleeting days,
I may be if I will, divine,
 Standing before God's throne in praise, --
Through all Eternity to shine
 In yonder Heaven's sapphire blaze.

Father, the soul that counts it gain
 To love Thee and Thy law on earth,
Unchanged but free from mortal stain,
 Increased in knowledge and in worth,
And purified from this world's pain,
 Shall find through Thee a second birth.

A change! no surely not a change!
 The change must be before we die;
Death may confer a wider range
 From world to world, from sky to sky,
It cannot make me new or strange
 To mine own Personality!

Daniel Henry Deniehy.

Love in a Cottage

A cottage small be mine, with porch

Enwreathed with ivy green,
And brightsome flowers with dew-filled bells,
'Mid brown old wattles seen.

And one to wait at shut of eve,
 With eyes as fountain clear,
And braided hair, and simple dress,
 My homeward step to hear.

On summer eves to sing old songs,
 And talk o'er early vows,
While stars look down like angels' eyes
 Amid the leafy boughs.

When Spring flowers peep from flossy cells,
 And bright-winged parrots call,
In forest paths be ours to rove
 Till purple evenings fall.

The curtains closed, by taper clear
 To read some page divine,
On winter nights, the hearth beside,
 Her soft, warm hand in mine.

And so to glide through busy life,
 Like some small brook alone,
That winds its way 'mid grassy knolls,
 Its music all its own.

A Song for the Night

O the Night, the Night, the solemn Night,
　When Earth is bound with her silent zone,
And the spangled sky seems a temple wide,
　Where the star-tribes kneel at the Godhead's throne;
O the Night, the Night, the wizard Night,
　When the garish reign of day is o'er,
And the myriad barques of the dream-elves come
　In a brightsome fleet from Slumber's shore!
　　　O the Night for me,
　　　When blithe and free,
Go the zephyr-hounds on their airy chase;
　　　When the moon is high
　　　In the dewy sky,
And the air is sweet as a bride's embrace!

O the Night, the Night, the charming Night!
　From the fountain side in the myrtle shade,
All softly creep on the slumbrous air
　The waking notes of the serenade;
While bright eyes shine 'mid the lattice-vines,
　And white arms droop o'er the sculptured sills,
And accents fall to the knights below,
　Like the babblings soft of mountain rills.
　　　Love in their eyes,
　　　Love in their sighs,
Love in the heave of each lily-bright bosom;
　　　In words so clear,
　　　Lest the listening ear
And the waiting heart may lose them.

O the silent Night, when the student dreams
 Of kneeling crowds round a sage's tomb;
And the mother's eyes o'er the cradle rain
 Tears for her baby's fading bloom;
O the peaceful Night, when stilled and o'er
 Is the charger's tramp on the battle plain,
And the bugle's sound and the sabre's flash,
 While the moon looks sad over heaps of slain;
    And tears bespeak
    On the iron cheek
Of the sentinel lonely pacing,
    Thoughts which roll
    Through his fearless soul,
Day's sterner mood replacing.

O the sacred Night, when memory comes
 With an aspect mild and sweet to me,
But her tones are sad as a ballad air
 In childhood heard on a nurse's knee;
And round her throng fair forms long fled,
 With brows of snow and hair of gold,
And eyes with the light of summer skies,
 And lips that speak of the days of old.
    Wide is your flight,
    O spirits of Night,
By strath, and stream, and grove,
    But most in the gloom
    Of the Poet's room
Ye choose, fair ones, to rove.

Richard Rowe.

Superstites Rosae

The grass is green upon her grave,
 The west wind whispers low;
"The corn is changed, come forth, come forth,
 Ere all the blossoms go!"

In vain. Her laughing eyes are sealed,
 And cold her sunny brow;
Last year she smiled upon the flowers --
 They smile above her now!

Soul Ferry

High and dry upon the shingle lies the fisher's boat to-night;
From his roof-beam dankly drooping, raying phosphorescent light,
Spectral in its pale-blue splendour, hangs his heap of scaly nets,
And the fisher, lapt in slumber, surge and seine alike forgets.

Hark! there comes a sudden knocking, and the fisher starts from sleep,
As a hollow voice and ghostly bids him once more seek the deep;

Wearily across his shoulder flingeth he the ashen oar,
And upon the beach descending finds a skiff beside the shore.

'Tis not his, but he must enter -- rocking on the waters dim,
Awful in their hidden presence, who are they that wait for him?
Who are they that sit so silent, as he pulleth from the land --
Nothing heard save rumbling rowlock, wave soft-breaking on the sand?

Chill adown the tossing channel blows the wailing, wand'ring breeze,
Lonely in the murky midnight, mutt'ring mournful memories, --
Summer lands where once it brooded, wrecks that widows' hearts have wrung --
Swift the dreary boat flies onwards, spray, like rain, around it flung.

On a pebbled strand it grateth, ghastly cliffs around it loom,
Thin and melancholy voices faintly murmur through the gloom;
Voices only, lipless voices, and the fisherman turns pale,
As the mother greets her children, sisters landing brothers hail.

Lightened of its unseen burden, cork-like rides the rocking bark,
Fast the fisherman flies homewards o'er the billows deep and dark;
THAT boat needs no mortal's mooring -- sad at heart he seeks his bed,
For his life henceforth is clouded -- he hath piloted the Dead!

Sir Henry Parkes.

The Buried Chief

(November 6th, 1886)

With speechless lips and solemn tread
  They brought the Lawyer-Statesman home:
They laid him with the gather'd dead,
  Where rich and poor like brothers come.

How bravely did the stripling climb,
  From step to step the rugged hill:
His gaze thro' that benighted time
  Fix'd on the far-off beacon still.

He faced the storm that o'er him burst,
  With pride to match the proudest born:
He bore unblench'd Detraction's worst, --
  Paid blow for blow, and scorn for scorn.

He scaled the summit while the sun
  Yet shone upon his conquer'd track:
Nor falter'd till the goal was won,
  Nor struggling upward, once look'd back.

But what avails the "pride of place",
 Or winged chariot rolling past?
He heeds not now who wins the race,
 Alike to him the first or last.

Thomas Alexander Browne (`Rolf Boldrewood').

Perdita

She is beautiful yet, with her wondrous hair
 And eyes that are stormy with fitful light,
The delicate hues of brow and cheek
 Are unmarred all, rose-clear and bright;
That matchless frame yet holds at bay
The crouching bloodhounds, Remorse, Decay.

There is no fear in her great dark eyes --
 No hope, no love, no care,
Stately and proud she looks around
 With a fierce, defiant stare;
Wild words deform her reckless speech,
Her laugh has a sadness tears never reach.

Whom should she fear on earth? Can Fate
 One direr torment lend

To her few little years of glitter and gloom
 With the sad old story to end
When the spectres of Loneliness, Want and Pain
Shall arise one night with Death in their train?

. . . . .

I see in a vision a woman like her
 Trip down an orchard slope,
With rosy prattlers that shout a name
 In tones of rapture and hope;
While the yeoman, gazing at children and wife,
Thanks God for the pride and joy of his life.

. . . . .

Whose conscience is heavy with this dark guilt?
 Who pays at the final day
For a wasted body, a murdered soul,
 And how shall he answer, I say,
For her outlawed years, her early doom,
And despair -- despair -- beyond the tomb?

Adam Lindsay Gordon.

A Dedication

They are rhymes rudely strung with intent less
   Of sound than of words,
In lands where bright blossoms are scentless,
   And songless bright birds;
Where, with fire and fierce drought on her tresses,
Insatiable summer oppresses
Sere woodlands and sad wildernesses,
   And faint flocks and herds.

Where in dreariest days, when all dews end,
   And all winds are warm,
Wild Winter's large flood-gates are loosen'd,
   And floods, freed from storm,
From broken-up fountain heads, dash on
Dry deserts with long pent up passion --
Here rhyme was first framed without fashion --
   Song shaped without form.

Whence gather'd? -- The locust's glad chirrup
   May furnish a stave;
The ring of a rowel and stirrup,
   The wash of a wave;

The chaunt of the marsh frog in rushes,
That chimes through the pauses and hushes
Of nightfall, the torrent that gushes,
   The tempests that rave;

In the deep'ning of dawn, when it dapples
   The dusk of the sky,
With streaks like the redd'ning of apples,
   The ripening of rye.
To eastward, when cluster by cluster,
Dim stars and dull planets, that muster,
Wax wan in a world of white lustre
   That spreads far and high;

In the gathering of night gloom o'erhead, in
   The still silent change,
All fire-flush'd when forest trees redden
   On slopes of the range.
When the gnarl'd, knotted trunks Eucalyptian
Seem carved, like weird columns Egyptian,
With curious device, quaint inscription,
   And hieroglyph strange;

In the Spring, when the wattle gold trembles
   'Twixt shadow and shine,
When each dew-laden air draught resembles
   A long draught of wine;
When the sky-line's blue burnish'd resistance
Makes deeper the dreamiest distance,
Some song in all hearts hath existence, --
   Such songs have been mine.

Thora's Song

We severed in Autumn early,
 Ere the earth was torn by the plough;
The wheat and the oats and the barley
 Are ripe for the harvest now.
We sunder'd one misty morning
 Ere the hills were dimm'd by the rain;
Through the flowers those hills adorning --
 Thou comest not back again.

My heart is heavy and weary
 With the weight of a weary soul;
The mid-day glare grows dreary,
 And dreary the midnight scroll.
The corn-stalks sigh for the sickle,
 'Neath the load of their golden grain;
I sigh for a mate more fickle --
 Thou comest not back again.

The warm sun riseth and setteth,
 The night bringeth moistening dew,
But the soul that longeth forgetteth
 The warmth and the moisture too.
In the hot sun rising and setting
 There is naught save feverish pain;
There are tears in the night-dews wetting --
 Thou comest not back again.

Thy voice in my ear still mingles
 With the voices of whisp'ring trees,

Thy kiss on my cheek still tingles
  At each kiss of the summer breeze.
While dreams of the past are thronging
  For substance of shades in vain,
I am waiting, watching and longing --
  Thou comest not back again.

Waiting and watching ever,
  Longing and lingering yet;
Leaves rustle and corn-stalks quiver,
  Winds murmur and waters fret.
No answer they bring, no greeting,
  No speech, save that sad refrain,
Nor voice, save an echo repeating --
  He cometh not back again.

The Sick Stock-rider

Hold hard, Ned! Lift me down once more, and lay me in the shade.
  Old man, you've had your work cut out to guide
Both horses, and to hold me in the saddle when I swayed,
  All through the hot, slow, sleepy, silent ride.
The dawn at "Moorabinda" was a mist rack dull and dense,
  The sun-rise was a sullen, sluggish lamp;
I was dozing in the gateway at Arbuthnot's bound'ry fence,
  I was dreaming on the Limestone cattle camp.
We crossed the creek at Carricksford, and sharply through the haze,
  And suddenly the sun shot flaming forth;
To southward lay "Katawa", with the sand peaks all ablaze,
  And the flushed fields of Glen Lomond lay to north.

Now westward winds the bridle-path that leads to Lindisfarm,
  And yonder looms the double-headed Bluff;
From the far side of the first hill, when the skies are clear and calm,
  You can see Sylvester's woolshed fair enough.
Five miles we used to call it from our homestead to the place
  Where the big tree spans the roadway like an arch;
'Twas here we ran the dingo down that gave us such a chase
  Eight years ago -- or was it nine? -- last March.
'Twas merry in the glowing morn among the gleaming grass,
  To wander as we've wandered many a mile,
And blow the cool tobacco cloud, and watch the white wreaths pass,
  Sitting loosely in the saddle all the while.
'Twas merry 'mid the blackwoods, when we spied the station roofs,
  To wheel the wild scrub cattle at the yard,
With a running fire of stock whips and a fiery run of hoofs;
  Oh! the hardest day was never then too hard!
Aye! we had a glorious gallop after "Starlight" and his gang,
  When they bolted from Sylvester's on the flat;
How the sun-dried reed-beds crackled, how the flint-strewn ranges rang,
  To the strokes of "Mountaineer" and "Acrobat".
Hard behind them in the timber, harder still across the heath,
  Close beside them through the tea-tree scrub we dash'd;
And the golden-tinted fern leaves, how they rustled underneath;
  And the honeysuckle osiers, how they crash'd!
We led the hunt throughout, Ned, on the chestnut and the grey,
  And the troopers were three hundred yards behind,
While we emptied our six-shooters on the bushrangers at bay,
  In the creek with stunted box-trees for a blind!
There you grappled with the leader, man to man, and horse to horse,
  And you roll'd together when the chestnut rear'd;
He blazed away and missed you in that shallow water-course --
  A narrow shave -- his powder singed your beard!

In these hours when life is ebbing, how those days when life was young
  Come back to us; how clearly I recall
Even the yarns Jack Hall invented, and the songs Jem Roper sung;
  And where are now Jem Roper and Jack Hall?
Ay! nearly all our comrades of the old colonial school,
  Our ancient boon companions, Ned, are gone;
Hard livers for the most part, somewhat reckless as a rule,
  It seems that you and I are left alone.
There was Hughes, who got in trouble through that business with the cards,
  It matters little what became of him;
But a steer ripp'd up Macpherson in the Cooraminta yards,
  And Sullivan was drown'd at Sink-or-swim;
And Mostyn -- poor Frank Mostyn -- died at last, a fearful wreck,
  In the "horrors" at the Upper Wandinong,
And Carisbrooke, the rider, at the Horsefall broke his neck;
  Faith! the wonder was he saved his neck so long!

Ah! those days and nights we squandered at the Logans' in the glen --
  The Logans, man and wife, have long been dead.
Elsie's tallest girl seems taller than your little Elsie then;
  And Ethel is a woman grown and wed.

I've had my share of pastime, and I've done my share of toil,
  And life is short -- the longest life a span;
I care not now to tarry for the corn or for the oil,
  Or for wine that maketh glad the heart of man.
For good undone, and gifts misspent, and resolutions vain,
  'Tis somewhat late to trouble. This I know --
I should live the same life over, if I had to live again;
  And the chances are I go where most men go.

The deep blue skies wax dusky, and the tall green trees grow dim,
  The sward beneath me seems to heave and fall;

And sickly, smoky shadows through the sleepy sunlight swim,
 And on the very sun's face weave their pall.
Let me slumber in the hollow where the wattle blossoms wave,
 With never stone or rail to fence my bed;
Should the sturdy station children pull the bush-flowers on my grave,
 I may chance to hear them romping overhead.

I don't suppose I shall though, for I feel like sleeping sound,
 That sleep, they say, is doubtful. True; but yet
At least it makes no difference to the dead man underground
 What the living men remember or forget.
Enigmas that perplex us in the world's unequal strife,
 The future may ignore or may reveal;
Yet some, as weak as water, Ned, to make the best of life,
 Have been to face the worst as true as steel.

Henry Kendall.

Prefatory Sonnets

I.

I purposed once to take my pen and write,

Not songs, like some, tormented and awry
 With passion, but a cunning harmony
Of words and music caught from glen and height,
And lucid colours born of woodland light
 And shining places where the sea-streams lie.
But this was when the heat of youth glowed white,
 And since I've put the faded purpose by.
I have no faultless fruits to offer you
 Who read this book; but certain syllables
 Herein are borrowed from unfooted dells
And secret hollows dear to noontide dew;
And these at least, though far between and few,
 May catch the sense like subtle forest spells.

   II.

So take these kindly, even though there be
 Some notes that unto other lyres belong,
 Stray echoes from the elder sons of song;
And think how from its neighbouring native sea
The pensive shell doth borrow melody.
 I would not do the lordly masters wrong
 By filching fair words from the shining throng
Whose music haunts me as the wind a tree!
 Lo, when a stranger in soft Syrian glooms
Shot through with sunset treads the cedar dells,
And hears the breezy ring of elfin bells
 Far down by where the white-haired cataract booms,
He, faint with sweetness caught from forest smells,
 Bears thence, unwitting, plunder of perfumes.

September in Australia

Grey Winter hath gone, like a wearisome guest,
   And, behold, for repayment,
September comes in with the wind of the West
   And the Spring in her raiment!
The ways of the frost have been filled of the flowers,
   While the forest discovers
Wild wings, with the halo of hyaline hours,
   And the music of lovers.

September, the maid with the swift, silver feet!
   She glides, and she graces
The valleys of coolness, the slopes of the heat,
   With her blossomy traces;
Sweet month, with a mouth that is made of a rose,
   She lightens and lingers
In spots where the harp of the evening glows,
   Attuned by her fingers.

The stream from its home in the hollow hill slips
   In a darling old fashion;
And the day goeth down with a song on its lips
   Whose key-note is passion;
Far out in the fierce, bitter front of the sea
   I stand, and remember
Dead things that were brothers and sisters of thee,
   Resplendent September.

The West, when it blows at the fall of the noon
   And beats on the beaches,

Is filled with a tender and tremulous tune
   That touches and teaches;
The stories of Youth, of the burden of Time,
   And the death of Devotion,
Come back with the wind, and are themes of the rhyme
   In the waves of the ocean.

We, having a secret to others unknown,
   In the cool mountain-mosses,
May whisper together, September, alone
   Of our loves and our losses.
One word for her beauty, and one for the grace
   She gave to the hours;
And then we may kiss her, and suffer her face
   To sleep with the flowers.

     . . . . .

Oh, season of changes -- of shadow and shine --
   September the splendid!
My song hath no music to mingle with thine,
   And its burden is ended;
But thou, being born of the winds and the sun,
   By mountain, by river,
Mayst lighten and listen, and loiter and run,
   With thy voices for ever.

Rose Lorraine

Sweet water-moons, blown into lights

Of flying gold on pool and creek,
And many sounds and many sights
 Of younger days are back this week.
I cannot say I sought to face
 Or greatly cared to cross again
The subtle spirit of the place
 Whose life is mixed with Rose Lorraine.

What though her voice rings clearly through
 A nightly dream I gladly keep,
No wish have I to start anew
 Heart fountains that have ceased to leap.
Here, face to face with different days,
 And later things that plead for love,
It would be worse than wrong to raise
 A phantom far too vain to move.

But, Rose Lorraine -- ah! Rose Lorraine,
 I'll whisper now, where no one hears --
If you should chance to meet again
 The man you kissed in soft, dead years,
Just say for once "He suffered much,"
 And add to this "His fate was worst
Because of me, my voice, my touch" --
 There is no passion like the first!

If I that breathe your slow sweet name,
 As one breathes low notes on a flute,
Have vext your peace with word of blame,
 The phrase is dead -- the lips are mute.
Yet when I turn towards the wall,
 In stormy nights, in times of rain,
I often wish you could recall

Your tender speeches, Rose Lorraine.

Because, you see, I thought them true,
 And did not count you self-deceived,
And gave myself in all to you,
 And looked on Love as Life achieved.
Then came the bitter, sudden change,
 The fastened lips, the dumb despair:
The first few weeks were very strange,
 And long, and sad, and hard to bear.

No woman lives with power to burst
 My passion's bonds, and set me free;
For Rose is last where Rose was first,
 And only Rose is fair to me.
The faintest memory of her face,
 The wilful face that hurt me so,
Is followed by a fiery trace
 That Rose Lorraine must never know.

I keep a faded ribbon string
 You used to wear about your throat;
And of this pale, this perished thing,
 I think I know the threads by rote.
God help such love! To touch your hand,
 To loiter where your feet might fall,
You marvellous girl, my soul would stand
 The worst of hell -- its fires and all!

To a Mountain

To thee, O father of the stately peaks,
Above me in the loftier light -- to thee,
Imperial brother of those awful hills
Whose feet are set in splendid spheres of flame,
Whose heads are where the gods are, and whose sides
Of strength are belted round with all the zones
Of all the world, I dedicate these songs.
And if, within the compass of this book,
There lives and glows ONE verse in which there beats
The pulse of wind and torrent -- if ONE line
Is here that like a running water sounds,
And seems an echo from the lands of leaf,
Be sure that line is thine. Here, in this home,
Away from men and books and all the schools,
I take thee for my Teacher. In thy voice
Of deathless majesty, I, kneeling, hear
God's grand authentic Gospel! Year by year,
The great sublime cantata of thy storm
Strikes through my spirit -- fills it with a life
Of startling beauty! Thou my Bible art
With holy leaves of rock, and flower, and tree,
And moss, and shining runnel. From each page
That helps to make thy awful volume, I
Have learned a noble lesson. In the psalm
Of thy grave winds, and in the liturgy
Of singing waters, lo! my soul has heard
The higher worship; and from thee, indeed,
The broad foundations of a finer hope
Were gathered in; and thou hast lifted up

The blind horizon for a larger faith!
Moreover, walking in exalted woods
Of naked glory, in the green and gold
Of forest sunshine, I have paused like one
With all the life transfigured: and a flood
Of light ineffable has made me feel
As felt the grand old prophets caught away
By flames of inspiration; but the words
Sufficient for the story of my Dream
Are far too splendid for poor human lips!
But thou, to whom I turn with reverent eyes --
O stately Father, whose majestic face
Shines far above the zone of wind and cloud,
Where high dominion of the morning is --
Thou hast the Song complete of which my songs
Are pallid adumbrations! Certain sounds
Of strong authentic sorrow in this book
May have the sob of upland torrents -- these,
And only these, may touch the great World's heart;
For, lo! they are the issues of that grief
Which makes a man more human, and his life
More like that frank exalted life of thine.
But in these pages there are other tones
In which thy large, superior voice is not --
Through which no beauty that resembles thine
Has ever shone. THESE are the broken words
Of blind occasions, when the World has come
Between me and my Dream. No song is here
Of mighty compass; for my singing robes
I've worn in stolen moments. All my days
Have been the days of a laborious life,
And ever on my struggling soul has burned
The fierce heat of this hurried sphere. But thou,

To whose fair majesty I dedicate
My book of rhymes -- thou hast the perfect rest
Which makes the heaven of the highest gods!
To thee the noises of this violent time
Are far, faint whispers; and, from age to age,
Within the world and yet apart from it,
Thou standest! Round thy lordly capes the sea
Rolls on with a superb indifference
For ever; in thy deep, green, gracious glens
The silver fountains sing for ever. Far
Above dim ghosts of waters in the caves,
The royal robe of morning on thy head
Abides for ever! Evermore the wind
Is thy august companion; and thy peers
Are cloud, and thunder, and the face sublime
Of blue mid-heaven! On thy awful brow
Is Deity; and in that voice of thine
There is the great imperial utterance
Of God for ever; and thy feet are set
Where evermore, through all the days and years,
There rolls the grand hymn of the deathless wave.

Araluen

Take this rose, and very gently place it on the tender, deep
Mosses where our little darling, Araluen, lies asleep.
Put the blossom close to baby -- kneel with me, my love, and pray;
We must leave the bird we've buried -- say good-bye to her to-day;
In the shadow of our trouble we must go to other lands,
And the flowers we have fostered will be left to other hands.

Other eyes will watch them growing -- other feet will softly tread
Where two hearts are nearly breaking, where so many tears are shed.
Bitter is the world we live in: life and love are mixed with pain;
We will never see these daisies -- never water them again.
. . . . .
Here the blue-eyed Spring will linger, here the shining month will stay,
Like a friend, by Araluen, when we two are far away;
But, beyond the wild, wide waters, we will tread another shore --
We will never watch this blossom, never see it any more.

Girl, whose hand at God's high altar in the dear, dead year I pressed,
Lean your stricken head upon me -- this is still your lover's breast!
She who sleeps was first and sweetest -- none we have to take her place!
Empty is the little cradle -- absent is the little face.
Other children may be given; but this rose beyond recall,
But this garland of your girlhood, will be dearest of them all.
None will ever, Araluen, nestle where you used to be,
In my heart of hearts, you darling, when the world was new to me;
We were young when you were with us, life and love were happy things
To your father and your mother ere the angels gave you wings.

You that sit and sob beside me -- you, upon whose golden head
Many rains of many sorrows have from day to day been shed;
Who, because your love was noble, faced with me the lot austere
Ever pressing with its hardship on the man of letters here --
Let me feel that you are near me, lay your hand within mine own;
You are all I have to live for, now that we are left alone.
Three there were, but one has vanished. Sins of mine have made you weep;
But forgive your baby's father now that baby is asleep.
Let us go, for night is falling, leave the darling with her flowers;
Other hands will come and tend them -- other friends in other hours.

After Many Years

The song that once I dreamed about,
 The tender, touching thing,
As radiant as the rose without,
 The love of wind and wing:
The perfect verses, to the tune
 Of woodland music set,
As beautiful as afternoon,
 Remain unwritten yet.

It is too late to write them now --
 The ancient fire is cold;
No ardent lights illume the brow,
 As in the days of old.
I cannot dream the dream again;
 But, when the happy birds
Are singing in the sunny rain,
 I think I hear its words.

I think I hear the echo still
 Of long-forgotten tones,
When evening winds are on the hill
 And sunset fires the cones;
But only in the hours supreme,
 With songs of land and sea,
The lyrics of the leaf and stream,
 This echo comes to me.

No longer doth the earth reveal
 Her gracious green and gold;

I sit where youth was once, and feel
 That I am growing old.
The lustre from the face of things
 Is wearing all away;
Like one who halts with tired wings,
 I rest and muse to-day.

There is a river in the range
 I love to think about;
Perhaps the searching feet of change
 Have never found it out.
Ah! oftentimes I used to look
 Upon its banks, and long
To steal the beauty of that brook
 And put it in a song.

I wonder if the slopes of moss,
 In dreams so dear to me --
The falls of flower, and flower-like floss --
 Are as they used to be!
I wonder if the waterfalls,
 The singers far and fair,
That gleamed between the wet, green walls,
 Are still the marvels there!

Ah! let me hope that in that place
 Those old familiar things
To which I turn a wistful face
 Have never taken wings.
Let me retain the fancy still
 That, past the lordly range,
There always shines, in folds of hill,
 One spot secure from change!

I trust that yet the tender screen
  That shades a certain nook
Remains, with all its gold and green,
  The glory of the brook.
It hides a secret to the birds
  And waters only known:
The letters of two lovely words --
  A poem on a stone.

Perhaps the lady of the past
  Upon these lines may light,
The purest verses, and the last,
  That I may ever write:
She need not fear a word of blame:
  Her tale the flowers keep --
The wind that heard me breathe her name
  Has been for years asleep.

But in the night, and when the rain
  The troubled torrent fills,
I often think I see again
  The river in the hills;
And when the day is very near,
  And birds are on the wing,
My spirit fancies it can hear
  The song I cannot sing.

Hy-Brasil

"Daughter," said the ancient father, pausing by the evening sea,
"Turn thy face towards the sunset -- turn thy face and kneel with me!
Prayer and praise and holy fasting, lips of love and life of light,
These and these have made thee perfect -- shining saint with seraph's sight!
Look towards that flaming crescent -- look beyond that glowing space --
Tell me, sister of the angels, what is beaming in thy face?"
And the daughter, who had fasted, who had spent her days in prayer,
Till the glory of the Saviour touched her head and rested there,
Turned her eyes towards the sea-line -- saw beyond the fiery crest,
Floating over waves of jasper, far Hy-Brasil in the West.

All the calmness and the colour -- all the splendour and repose,
Flowing where the sunset flowered, like a silver-hearted rose!
There indeed was singing Eden, where the great gold river runs
Past the porch and gates of crystal, ringed by strong and shining ones!
There indeed was God's own garden, sailing down the sapphire sea --
Lawny dells and slopes of summer, dazzling stream and radiant tree!
Out against the hushed horizon -- out beneath the reverent day,
Flamed the Wonder on the waters -- flamed, and flashed, and passed away.
And the maiden who had seen it felt a hand within her own,
And an angel that we know not led her to the lands unknown.

Never since hath eye beheld it -- never since hath mortal, dazed
By its strange, unearthly splendour, on the floating Eden gazed!
Only once since Eve went weeping through a throng of glittering wings,
Hath the holy seen Hy-Brasil where the great gold river sings!
Only once by quiet waters, under still, resplendent skies,
Did the sister of the seraphs kneel in sight of Paradise!
She, the pure, the perfect woman, sanctified by patient prayer,

Had the eyes of saints of Heaven, all their glory in her hair:
Therefore God the Father whispered to a radiant spirit near --
"Show Our daughter fair Hy-Brasil -- show her this, and lead her here."

But beyond the halls of sunset, but within the wondrous West,
On the rose-red seas of evening, sails the Garden of the Blest.
Still the gates of glassy beauty, still the walls of glowing light,
Shine on waves that no man knows of, out of sound and out of sight.
Yet the slopes and lawns of lustre, yet the dells of sparkling streams,
Dip to tranquil shores of jasper, where the watching angel beams.
But, behold! our eyes are human, and our way is paved with pain,
We can never find Hy-Brasil, never see its hills again!
Never look on bays of crystal, never bend the reverent knee
In the sight of Eden floating -- floating on the sapphire sea!

Outre Mer

I see, as one in dreaming,
 A broad, bright, quiet sea;
Beyond it lies a haven --
 The only home for me.
Some men grow strong with trouble,
 But all my strength is past,
And tired and full of sorrow,
 I long to sleep at last.
By force of chance and changes
 Man's life is hard at best;
And, seeing rest is voiceless,
 The dearest thing is rest.

Beyond the sea -- behold it,
 The home I wish to seek,
The refuge of the weary,
 The solace of the weak!
Sweet angel fingers beckon,
 Sweet angel voices ask
My soul to cross the waters;
 And yet I dread the task.
God help the man whose trials
 Are tares that he must reap!
He cannot face the future --
 His only hope is sleep.

Across the main a vision
 Of sunset coasts, and skies,
And widths of waters gleaming,
 Enchant my human eyes.
I, who have sinned and suffered,
 Have sought -- with tears have sought --
To rule my life with goodness,
 And shape it to my thought.
And yet there is no refuge
 To shield me from distress,
Except the realm of slumber
 And great forgetfulness.

Marcus Clarke.

The Song of Tigilau

The song of Tigilau the brave,
  Sina's wild lover,
Who across the heaving wave
  From Samoa came over:
Came over, Sina, at the setting moon!

The moon shines round and bright;
  She, with her dark-eyed maidens at her side,
  Watches the rising tide.
While balmy breathes the starry southern night,
While languid heaves the lazy southern tide;
The rising tide, O Sina, and the setting moon!

The night is past, is past and gone,
  The moon sinks to the West,
  The sea-heart beats opprest,
  And Sina's passionate breast
Heaves like the sea, when the pale moon has gone,
Heaves like the passionate sea, Sina, left by the moon alone!

Silver on silver sands, the rippling waters meet --
  Will he come soon?

The rippling waters kiss her delicate feet,
The rippling waters, lisping low and sweet,
   Ripple with the tide,
    The rising tide,
The rising tide, O Sina, and the setting moon!

He comes! -- her lover!
Tigilau, the son of Tui Viti.
Her maidens round her hover,
The rising waves her white feet cover.
   O Tigilau, son of Tui Viti,
   Through the mellow dusk thy proas glide,
    So soon!
   So soon by the rising tide,
The rising tide, my Sina, and the setting moon!

The mooring-poles are left,
The whitening waves are cleft,
   By the prows of Tui Viti!
   By the sharp keels of Tui Viti!
Broad is the sea, and deep,
The yellow Samoans sleep,
 But they will wake and weep --
Weep in their luxurious odorous vales,
While the land breeze swells the sails
    Of Tui Viti!
 Tui Viti -- far upon the rising tide,
    The rising tide --
The rising tide, my Sina, beneath the setting moon!

She leaps to meet him!
Her mouth to greet him
  Burns at his own.

Away! To the canoes,
To the yoked war canoes!
　The sea in murmurous tone
Whispers the story of their loves,
Re-echoes the story of their loves --
　The story of Tui Viti,
　Of Sina and Tui Viti,
　By the rising tide,
The rising tide, Sina, beneath the setting moon!

　　She has gone!
　　She has fled!
　　　Sina!
Sina, for whom the warriors decked their shining hair,
Wreathing with pearls their bosoms brown and bare,
Flinging beneath her dainty feet
Mats crimson with the feathers of the parrakeet.
　Ho, Samoans! rouse your warriors full soon,
　For Sina is across the rippling wave,
　　With Tigilau, the bold and brave.
　Far, far upon the rising tide!
　Far upon the rising tide!
Far upon the rising tide, Sina, beneath the setting moon.

Patrick Moloney.

Melbourne

O sweet Queen-city of the golden South,
  Piercing the evening with thy star-lit spires,
Thou wert a witness when I kissed the mouth
  Of her whose eyes outblazed the skyey fires.
I saw the parallels of thy long streets,
  With lamps like angels shining all a-row,
While overhead the empyrean seats
  Of gods were steeped in paradisic glow.
The Pleiades with rarer fires were tipt,
  Hesper sat throned upon his jewelled chair,
The belted giant's triple stars were dipt
  In all the splendour of Olympian air,
On high to bless, the Southern Cross did shine,
Like that which blazed o'er conquering Constantine.

Alfred Domett.

An Invitation

Well! if Truth be all welcomed with hardy reliance,
All the lovely unfoldings of luminous Science,
 All that Logic can prove or disprove be avowed:
Is there room for no faith -- though such Evil intrude --
In the dominance still of a Spirit of Good?
Is there room for no hope -- such a handbreadth we scan --
In the permanence yet of the Spirit of Man? --
 May we bless the far seeker, nor blame the fine dreamer?
  Leave Reason her radiance -- Doubt her due cloud;
    Nor their Rainbows enshroud? --

From our Life of realities -- hard -- shallow-hearted,
Has Romance -- has all glory idyllic departed --
 From the workaday World all the wonderment flown?
Well, but what if there gleamed, in an Age cold as this,
The divinest of Poets' ideal of bliss?
Yea, an Eden could lurk in this Empire of ours,
With the loneliest love in the loveliest bowers? --
 In an era so rapid with railway and steamer,
  And with Pan and the Dryads like Raphael gone --
    What if this could be shown?

O my friends, never deaf to the charms of Denial,
Were its comfortless comforting worth a life-trial --
 Discontented content with a chilling despair? --
Better ask as we float down a song-flood unchecked,
If our Sky with no Iris be glory-bedecked?
Through the gloom of eclipse as we wistfully steal
If no darkling aureolar rays may reveal
 That the Future is haply not utterly cheerless:
  While the Present has joy and adventure as rare
   As the Past when most fair?

And if weary of mists you will roam undisdaining
To a land where the fanciful fountains are raining
 Swift brilliants of boiling and beautiful spray
In the violet splendour of skies that illume
Such a wealth of green ferns and rare crimson tree-bloom;
Where a people primeval is vanishing fast,
With its faiths and its fables and ways of the past:
 O with reason and fancy unfettered and fearless,
  Come plunge with us deep into regions of Day --
   Come away -- and away! --

A Maori Girl's Song

"Alas, and well-a-day! they are talking of me still:
By the tingling of my nostril, I fear they are talking ill;
Poor hapless I -- poor little I -- so many mouths to fill --
 And all for this strange feeling -- O, this sad, sweet pain!

"O! senseless heart -- O simple! to yearn so, and to pine

For one so far above me, confest o'er all to shine,
For one a hundred dote upon, who never can be mine!
 O, 'tis a foolish feeling -- all this fond, sweet pain!

"When I was quite a child -- not so many moons ago --
A happy little maiden -- O, then it was not so;
Like a sunny-dancing wavelet then I sparkled to and fro;
 And I never had this feeling -- O, this sad, sweet pain!

"I think it must be owing to the idle life I lead
In the dreamy house for ever that this new bosom-weed
Has sprouted up and spread its shoots till it troubles me indeed
 With a restless, weary feeling -- such a sad, sweet pain!

"So in this pleasant islet, O, no longer will I stay --
And the shadowy summer dwelling I will leave this very day;
On Arapa I'll launch my skiff, and soon be borne away
 From all that feeds this feeling -- O, this fond, sweet pain!

"I'll go and see dear Rima -- she'll welcome me, I know,
And a flaxen cloak -- her gayest -- o'er my weary shoulders throw,
With purfle red and points so free -- O, quite a lovely show --
 To charm away this feeling -- O, this sad, sweet pain!

"Two feathers I will borrow, and so gracefully I'll wear
Two feathers soft and snowy, for my long, black, lustrous hair.
Of the albatross's down they'll be -- O, how charming they'll look there --
 All to chase away this feeling -- O, this fond, sweet pain!

"Then the lads will flock around me with flattering talk all day --
And, with anxious little pinches, sly hints of love convey;
And I shall blush with happy pride to hear them, I daresay,
 And quite forget this feeling -- O, this sad, sweet pain!"

James Brunton Stephens.

The Dominion of Australia

(A Forecast, 1877)

She is not yet; but he whose ear
Thrills to that finer atmosphere
 Where footfalls of appointed things,
 Reverberant of days to be,
 Are heard in forecast echoings,
 Like wave-beats from a viewless sea --
Hears in the voiceful tremors of the sky
Auroral heralds whispering, "She is nigh."

She is not yet; but he whose sight
Foreknows the advent of the light,
 Whose soul to morning radiance turns
 Ere night her curtain hath withdrawn,
 And in its quivering folds discerns
 The mute monitions of the dawn,
With urgent sense strained onward to descry
Her distant tokens, starts to find Her nigh.

Not yet her day. How long "not yet"? . . .
There comes the flush of violet!
 And heavenward faces, all aflame
  With sanguine imminence of morn,
 Wait but the sun-kiss to proclaim
  The Day of The Dominion born.
Prelusive baptism! -- ere the natal hour
Named with the name and prophecy of power.

 Already here to hearts intense,
 A spirit-force, transcending sense,
  In heights unscaled, in deeps unstirred,
   Beneath the calm, above the storm,
  She waits the incorporating word
   To bid her tremble into form.
Already, like divining-rods, men's souls
Bend down to where the unseen river rolls; --

 For even as, from sight concealed,
 By never flush of dawn revealed,
  Nor e'er illumed by golden noon,
   Nor sunset-streaked with crimson bar,
  Nor silver-spanned by wake of moon,
   Nor visited of any star,
Beneath these lands a river waits to bless
(So men divine) our utmost wilderness, --

 Rolls dark, but yet shall know our skies,
 Soon as the wisdom of the wise
  Conspires with nature to disclose
   The blessing prisoned and unseen,
  Till round our lessening wastes there glows

A perfect zone of broadening green, --
Till all our land, Australia Felix called,
Become one Continent-Isle of Emerald;

  So flows beneath our good and ill
  A viewless stream of Common Will,
   A gathering force, a present might,
    That from its silent depths of gloom
    At Wisdom's voice shall leap to light,
     And hide our barren feuds in bloom,
Till, all our sundering lines with love o'ergrown,
Our bounds shall be the girdling seas alone.

The Dark Companion

There is an orb that mocked the lore of sages
 Long time with mystery of strange unrest;
The steadfast law that rounds the starry ages
 Gave doubtful token of supreme behest.

But they who knew the ways of God unchanging,
 Concluded some far influence unseen --
Some kindred sphere through viewless ethers ranging,
 Whose strong persuasions spanned the void between.

And knowing it alone through perturbation
 And vague disquiet of another star,
They named it, till the day of revelation,
 "The Dark Companion" -- darkly guessed afar.

But when, through new perfection of appliance,
 Faith merged at length in undisputed sight,
The mystic mover was revealed to science,
 No Dark Companion, but -- a speck of light.

No Dark Companion, but a sun of glory;
 No fell disturber, but a bright compeer;
The shining complement that crowned the story;
 The golden link that made the meaning clear.

Oh, Dark Companion, journeying ever by us,
 Oh, grim Perturber of our works and ways --
Oh, potent Dread, unseen, yet ever nigh us,
 Disquieting all the tenor of our days --

Oh, Dark Companion, Death, whose wide embraces
 O'ertake remotest change of clime and skies --
Oh, Dark Companion, Death, whose grievous traces
 Are scattered shreds of riven enterprise --

Thou, too, in this wise, when, our eyes unsealing,
 The clearer day shall change our faith to sight,
Shalt show thyself, in that supreme revealing,
 No Dark Companion, but a thing of light.

No ruthless wrecker of harmonious order;
 No alien heart of discord and caprice;
A beckoning light upon the Blissful Border;
 A kindred element of law and peace.

So, too, our strange unrest in this our dwelling,
 The trembling that thou joinest with our mirth,
Are but thy magnet-communings compelling

Our spirits farther from the scope of earth.

So, doubtless, when beneath thy potence swerving,
 'Tis that thou lead'st us by a path unknown,
Our seeming deviations all subserving
 The perfect orbit round the central throne.

 . . . . .

The night wind moans. The Austral wilds are round me.
 The loved who live -- ah, God! how few they are!
I looked above; and heaven in mercy found me
 This parable of comfort in a star.

Day

Linger, oh Sun, for a little, nor close yet this day of a million!
 Is there not glory enough in the rose-curtained halls of the West?
Hast thou no joy in the passion-hued folds of thy kingly pavilion?
 Why shouldst thou only pass through it? Oh rest thee a little while, rest!

Why should the Night come and take it, the wan Night that cannot enjoy it,
 Bringing pale argent for golden, and changing vermilion to grey?
Why should the Night come and shadow it, entering but to destroy it?
 Rest 'mid thy ruby-trailed splendours! Oh stay thee a little while, stay!

Rest thee at least a brief hour in it! 'Tis a right royal pavilion.
 Lo, there are thrones for high dalliance all gloriously canopied o'er!
 Lo, there are hangings of purple, and hangings of blue and vermilion,
 And there are fleeces of gold for thy feet on the diapered floor!

Linger, a little while linger. To-morrow my heart may not sing to thee:
 This shall be Yesterday, numbered with memories, folded away.
Now should my flesh-fettered soul be set free! I would soar to thee,
  cling to thee,
 And be thy rere-ward Aurora, pursuing the skirts of To-day!

Night

 Hark how the tremulous night-wind is passing in joy-laden sighs;
Soft through my window it comes, like the fanning of pinions angelic,
 Whispering to cease from myself, and look out on the infinite skies.

Out on the orb-studded night, and the crescent effulgence of Dian;
 Out on the far-gleaming star-dust that marks where the angels have trod;
Out on the gem-pointed Cross, and the glittering pomp of Orion,
 Flaming in measureless azure, the coronal jewels of God;

Luminous streams of delight in the silent immensity flowing,
 Journeying surgelessly on through impalpable ethers of peace.
How can I think of myself when infinitude o'er me is glowing,
 Glowing with tokens of love from the land where my sorrows shall cease?

Oh, summer-night of the South! Oh, sweet languor of zephyrs love-sighing!
 Oh, mighty circuit of shadowy solitude, holy and still!
Music scarce audible, echo-less harmony joyously dying,
 Dying in faint suspirations o'er meadow, and forest, and hill!

I must go forth and be part of it, part of the night and its gladness.
 But a few steps, and I pause on the marge of the shining lagoon.

Here then, at length, I have rest; and I lay down my burden of sadness,
　Kneeling alone 'neath the stars and the silvery arc of the moon.

Thomas Bracken.

Not Understood

Not understood, we move along asunder;
　Our paths grow wider as the seasons creep
Along the years; we marvel and we wonder
　Why life is life, and then we fall asleep
　　Not understood.

Not understood, we gather false impressions
　And hug them closer as the years go by;
Till virtues often seem to us transgressions;
　And thus men rise and fall, and live and die
　　Not understood.

Not understood! Poor souls with stunted vision
　Oft measure giants with their narrow gauge;
The poisoned shafts of falsehood and derision
　Are oft impelled 'gainst those who mould the age,
　　Not understood.

Not understood! The secret springs of action
  Which lie beneath the surface and the show,
Are disregarded; with self-satisfaction
  We judge our neighbours, and they often go
    Not understood.

Not understood! How trifles often change us!
  The thoughtless sentence and the fancied slight
Destroy long years of friendship, and estrange us,
  And on our souls there falls a freezing blight;
    Not understood.

Not understood! How many breasts are aching
  For lack of sympathy! Ah! day by day
How many cheerless, lonely hearts are breaking!
  How many noble spirits pass away,
    Not understood.

O God! that men would see a little clearer,
  Or judge less harshly where they cannot see!
O God! that men would draw a little nearer
  To one another, -- they'd be nearer Thee,
    And understood.

Spirit of Song

Where is thy dwelling-place? Echo of sweetness,
  Seraph of tenderness, where is thy home?
Angel of happiness, herald of fleetness,
  Thou hast the key of the star-blazon'd dome.

    Where lays that never end
    Up to God's throne ascend,
And our fond heart-wishes lovingly throng,
    Soaring with thee above,
    Bearer of truth and love,
Teacher of heaven's tongue -- Spirit of Song!

Euphony, born in the realms of the tearless,
 Mingling thy notes with the voices of Earth;
Wanting thee, all would be dreary and cheerless,
 Weaver of harmony, giver of mirth.
    Comfort of child and sage,
    With us in youth and age,
Soothing the weak and inspiring the strong,
    Illuming the blackest night,
    Making the day more bright,
Oh! thou art dear to us, Spirit of Song!

Oft in the springtime, sweet words of affection
 Are whispered by thee in thy tenderest tone,
And in the winter dark clouds of dejection
 By thee are dispelled till all sorrow has flown.
    Thou'rt with the zephyrs low,
    And with the brooklet's flow,
And with the feathered choir all the year long;
    Happy each child of thine,
    Blest with thy gifts divine,
Charming our senses, sweet Spirit of Song!

Ada Cambridge.

What of the Night?

To you, who look below,
 Where little candles glow --
Who listen in a narrow street,
Confused with noise of passing feet --

To you 'tis wild and dark;
 No light, no guide, no ark,
For travellers lost on moor and lea,
And ship-wrecked mariners at sea.

But they who stand apart,
 With hushed but wakeful heart --
They hear the lulling of the gale,
And see the dawn-rise faint and pale.

A dawn whereto they grope
 In trembling faith and hope,
If haply, brightening, it may cast
A gleam on path and goal at last.

Good-bye

Good-bye! -- 'tis like a churchyard bell -- good-bye!
 Poor weeping eyes! Poor head, bowed down with woe!
 Kiss me again, dear love, before you go.
Ah, me, how fast the precious moments fly!
      Good-bye! Good-bye!

We are like mourners when they stand and cry
 At open grave in wintry wind and rain.
 Yes, it is death. But you shall rise again --
Your sun return to this benighted sky.
      Good-bye! Good-bye!

The great physician, Time, shall pacify
 This parting anguish with another friend.
 Your heart is broken now, but it will mend.
Though it is death, yet still you will not die.
      Good-bye! Good-bye!

Dear heart! dear eyes! dear tongue, that cannot lie!
 Your love is true, your grief is deep and sore;
 But love will pass -- then you will grieve no more.
New love will come. Your tears will soon be dry.
      Good-bye! Good-bye!

The Virgin Martyr

Every wild she-bird has nest and mate in the warm April weather,
But a captive woman, made for love -- no mate, no nest has she.
In the spring of young desire, young men and maids are wed together,
And the happy mothers flaunt their bliss for all the world to see:
Nature's sacramental feast for these -- an empty board for me.

I, a young maid once, an old maid now, deposed, despised, forgotten --
I, like them have thrilled with passion and have dreamed of nuptial rest,
Of the trembling life within me of my children unbegotten,
Of a breathing new-born body to my yearning bosom prest,
Of the rapture of a little soft mouth drinking at my breast.

Time, that heals so many sorrows, keeps mine ever freshly aching;
Though my face is growing furrowed and my brown hair turning white,
Still I mourn my irremediable loss, asleep or waking --
Still I hear my son's voice calling "mother" in the dead of night,
And am haunted by my girl's eyes that will never see the light.

O my children that I might have had! my children, lost for ever!
O the goodly years that might have been -- now desolate and bare!
O malignant God or Fate, what have I done that I should never
Take my birthright like the others, take the crown that women wear,
And possess the common heritage to which all flesh is heir?

Honour

Me let the world disparage and despise --
 As one unfettered with its gilded chains,
 As one untempted by its sordid gains,
Its pleasant vice, its profitable lies;
Let Justice, blind and halt and maimed, chastise
 The rebel spirit surging in my veins,
 Let the Law deal me penalties and pains
And make me hideous in my neighbours' eyes.

But let me fall not in mine own esteem,
 By poor deceit or selfish greed debased.
  Let me be clean from secret stain and shame,
Know myself true, though false as hell I seem --
 Know myself worthy, howsoe'er disgraced --
  Know myself right, though every tongue should blame.

Despair

Alone! Alone! No beacon, far or near!
 No chart, no compass, and no anchor stay!
 Like melting fog the mirage melts away
In all-surrounding darkness, void and clear.
Drifting, I spread vain hands, and vainly peer
 And vainly call for pilot, -- weep and pray;
 Beyond these limits not the faintest ray

Shows distant coast whereto the lost may steer.

O what is life, if we must hold it thus
 As wind-blown sparks hold momentary fire?
  What are these gifts without the larger boon?
O what is art, or wealth, or fame to us
 Who scarce have time to know what we desire?
 O what is love, if we must part so soon?

Faith

And is the great cause lost beyond recall?
 Have all the hopes of ages come to naught?
 Is life no more with noble meaning fraught?
Is life but death, and love its funeral pall?
Maybe. And still on bended knees I fall,
 Filled with a faith no preacher ever taught.
 O God -- MY God -- by no false prophet wrought --
I believe still, in despite of it all!

Let go the myths and creeds of groping men.
 This clay knows naught -- the Potter understands.
I own that Power divine beyond my ken,
 And still can leave me in His shaping hands.
But, O my God, that madest me to feel,
Forgive the anguish of the turning wheel!

Alexander Bathgate.

The Clematis

Fair crown of stars of purest ray,
  Hung aloft on Mapau tree,
What floral beauties ye display,
  Stars of snowy purity;
Around the dark-leaved mapau's head
Unsullied garlands ye have spread.

Concealed were all thy beauties rare
  'Neath the dark umbrageous shade,
But still to gain the loftiest spray,
  Thy weak stem its efforts made;
Now, every obstacle o'ercome,
Thou smilest from thy leafy home.

That home secure, 'mid sombre leaves
  Yielded by thy stalwart spouse,
Helps thee to show thy fairy crown,
  Decorates his dusky boughs:
His strength, thy beauty, both unite
And form a picture to delight.

Fair flower, methinks thou dost afford
  Emblem of a perfect wife,

Whose work is hidden from the world,
 Till, perchance, her husband's life
Is by her influence beautified,
And this by others is descried.

Philip Joseph Holdsworth.

Quis Separabit?

All my life's short years had been stern and sterile --
 I stood like one whom the blasts blow back --
As with shipmen whirled through the straits of Peril,
 So fierce foes menaced my every track.

But I steeled my soul to a strong endeavour,
 I bared my brow as the sharp strokes fell,
And I said to my heart -- "Hope on! Hope ever:
 Have Courage -- Courage, and all is well."

Then, bright as the blood in my heart's rich chalice,
 O Blossom, Blossom! -- you came from far;
And life rang joy, till the World's loud malice
 Shrilled to the edge of our utmost star.

And I said: "On me let the rough storms hurtle,
 The great clouds gather and shroud my sun --
But you shall be Queen where the rose and myrtle
 Laugh with the year till the year is done."

So my Dream fell dead; and the fluctuant passion --
 The stress and strain of the past re-grew,
The world laughed on in its heedless fashion,
 But Earth whirled worthless, because of you!

In that Lake of Tears which my grief discovered,
 I laid dead Love with a passionate kiss,
And over those soundless depths has hovered
 The sweet, sad wraith of my vanished bliss.

Heart clings to Heart -- let the strange years sever
 The fates of two who had met -- to part;
Love's strength survives, and the harsh world never
 Shall crush the passion of heart for heart;

For I know my life, though it droop and dwindle,
 Shall leave me Love till I fade and die,
And when hereafter our Souls re-kindle,
 Who shall be fonder -- You or I?

My Queen of Dreams

In the warm flushed heart of the rose-red west,
 When the great sun quivered and died to-day,
You pulsed, O star, by yon pine-clad crest --

And throbbed till the bright eve ashened grey --
   Then I saw you swim
   By the shadowy rim
Where the grey gum dips to the western plain,
   And you rayed delight
   As you winged your flight
To the mystic spheres where your kinsmen reign.

O star, did you see her? My queen of dreams!
 Was it you that glimmered the night we strayed
A month ago by these scented streams?
 Half-checked by the litter the musk-buds made?
   Did you sleep or wake?
   Ah, for Love's sweet sake
(Though the world should fail and the soft stars wane!)
   I shall dream delight
   Till our souls take flight
To the mystic spheres where your kinsmen reign!

Mary Hannay Foott.

Where the Pelican Builds

The horses were ready, the rails were down,
 But the riders lingered still --

One had a parting word to say,
 And one had his pipe to fill.
Then they mounted, one with a granted prayer,
 And one with a grief unguessed.
  "We are going," they said, as they rode away --
 "Where the pelican builds her nest!"

They had told us of pastures wide and green,
 To be sought past the sunset's glow;
  Of rifts in the ranges by opal lit;
 And gold 'neath the river's flow.
And thirst and hunger were banished words
 When they spoke of that unknown West;
  No drought they dreaded, no flood they feared,
 Where the pelican builds her nest!

The creek at the ford was but fetlock deep
 When we watched them crossing there;
  The rains have replenished it thrice since then,
 And thrice has the rock lain bare.
But the waters of Hope have flowed and fled,
 And never from blue hill's breast
  Come back -- by the sun and the sands devoured --
 Where the pelican builds her nest.

New Country

Conde had come with us all the way --
 Eight hundred miles -- but the fortnight's rest
Made him fresh as a youngster, the sturdy bay!

And Lurline was looking her very best.

Weary and footsore, the cattle strayed
 'Mid the silvery saltbush well content;
Where the creeks lay cool 'neath the gidya's shade
 The stock-horses clustered, travel-spent.

In the bright spring morning we left them all --
 Camp, and cattle, and white, and black --
And rode for the Range's westward fall,
 Where the dingo's trail was the only track.

Slow through the clay-pans, wet to the knee,
 With the cane-grass rustling overhead;
Swift o'er the plains with never a tree;
 Up the cliffs by a torrent's bed.

Bridle on arm for a mile or more
 We toiled, ere we reached Bindanna's verge
And saw -- as one sees a far-off shore --
 The blue hills bounding the forest surge.

An ocean of trees, by the west wind stirred,
 Rolled, ever rolled, to the great cliff's base;
And its sound like the noise of waves was heard
 'Mid the rocks and the caves of that lonely place.

  . . . . .

We recked not of wealth in stream or soil
 As we heard on the heights the breezes sing;
We felt no longer our travel-toil;
 We feared no more what the years might bring.

No Message

She heard the story of the end,
　Each message, too, she heard;
And there was one for every friend;
　For her alone -- no word.

And shall she bear a heavier heart,
　And deem his love was fled;
Because his soul from earth could part
　Leaving her name unsaid?

No -- No! -- Though neither sign nor sound
　A parting thought expressed --
Not heedless passed the Homeward-Bound
　Of her he loved the best.

Of voyage-perils, bravely borne,
　He would not tell the tale;
Of shattered planks and canvas torn,
　And war with wind and gale.

He waited till the light-house star
　Should rise against the sky;
And from the mainland, looming far,
　The forest scents blow by.

He hoped to tell -- assurance sweet! --
　That pain and grief were o'er --

What blessings haste the soul to meet,
 Ere yet within the door.

Then one farewell he thought to speak
 When all the rest were past --
As in the parting-hour we seek
 The dearest hand the last.

And while for this delaying but
 To see Heaven's opening Gate --
Lo, it received him -- and was shut --
 Ere he could say "I wait."

Happy Days

A fringe of rushes -- one green line
 Upon a faded plain;
A silver streak of water-shine --
 Above, tree-watchers twain.
It was our resting-place awhile,
 And still, with backward gaze,
We say: "'Tis many a weary mile --
 But there were happy days."

And shall no ripple break the sand
 Upon our farther way?
Or reedy ranks all knee-deep stand?
 Or leafy tree-tops sway?
The gold of dawn is surely met
 In sunset's lavish blaze;

And -- in horizons hidden yet --
There shall be happy days.

Henry Lea Twisleton.

To a Cabbage Rose

Thy clustering leaves are steeped in splendour;
 No evening red, no morning dun,
Can show a hue as rich and tender
 As thine -- bright lover of the sun!

What wondrous hints of hidden glory,
 Of strains no human lips can sing;
What symbols rare of life's strange story,
 Dost thou from earth's dark bosom bring!

What elements have made thy sweetness,
 Thy glowing hue, thy emerald stem?
What hand has fashioned to completeness
 From tiny germ, thy diadem?

Thou art the fair earth's fond expression
 Of tenderness for heaven above --
The virgin blush that yields confession --

Thou bright "ambassador of love"!

Fair are thy leaves when summer glowing
  Lies in the lap of swooning spring;
But where art thou when autumn, blowing,
  Bids youth and tenderness take wing?

Sweet messenger! thou waftest beauty
  Wherever human lives are sown,
Around the peasant's humble duty
  Or weary grandeurs of a throne.

Transfused through hearts in future ages,
  Thy glowing power anew may shine
Effulgent in the poets' pages
  Or music's harmony divine.

But not to thee from future glory
  Can shine one added charm or day;
Sweet is thy life's unwritten story
  Of radiant bloom and swift decay.

Give, then, to vagrant winds thy sweetness,
  Shine, tearful, in the summer shower;
And, heedless of thy season's fleetness,
  Enrich with joy the passing hour.

Mrs. James Glenny Wilson.

Fairyland

Do you remember that careless band,
Riding o'er meadow and wet sea-sand,
 One autumn day, in a mist of sunshine,
Joyously seeking for fairyland?

The wind in the tree-tops was scarcely heard,
The streamlet repeated its one silver word,
 And far away, o'er the depths of wood-land,
Floated the bell of the parson-bird.

Pale hoar-frost glittered in shady slips,
Where ferns were dipping their finger-tips,
 From mossy branches a faint perfume
Breathed o'er honeyed Clematis lips.

At last we climbed to the ridge on high
Ah, crystal vision! Dreamland nigh!
 Far, far below us, the wide Pacific
Slumbered in azure from sky to sky.

And cloud and shadow, across the deep
Wavered, or paused in enchanted sleep,

And eastward, the purple-misted islets
Fretted the wave with terrace and steep.

We looked on the tranquil, glassy bay,
On headlands sheeted in dazzling spray,
 And the whitening ribs of a wreck forlorn
That for twenty years had wasted away.

All was so calm, and pure and fair,
It seemed the hour of worship there,
 Silent, as where the great North-Minster
Rises for ever, a visible prayer.

Then we turned from the murmurous forest-land,
And rode over shingle and silver sand,
 For so fair was the earth in the golden autumn,
That we sought no farther for Fairyland.

A Winter Daybreak

From the dark gorge, where burns the morning star,
 I hear the glacier river rattling on
And sweeping o'er his ice-ploughed shingle-bar,
 While wood owls shout in sombre unison,
 And fluttering southern dancers glide and go;
 And black swan's airy trumpets wildly, sweetly blow.

The cock crows in the windy winter morn,
 Then must I rise and fling the curtain by.
 All dark! But for a strip of fiery sky

Behind the ragged mountains, peaked and torn.
 One planet glitters in the icy cold,
Poised like a hawk above the frozen peaks,
And now again the wild nor'-wester speaks,
 And bends the cypress, shuddering, to his fold,
While every timber, every casement creaks.
 But still the skylarks sing aloud and bold;
The wooded hills arise; the white cascade
Shakes with wild laughter all the silent shadowy glade.

Now from the shuttered east a silvery bar
Shines through the mist, and shows the mild daystar.
 The storm-wrapped peaks start out and fade again,
 And rosy vapours skirt the pastoral plain;
The garden paths with hoary rime are wet;
And sweetly breathes the winter violet;
The jonquil half unfolds her ivory cup,
With clouds of gold-eyed daisies waking up.

Pleasant it is to turn and see the fire
Dance on the hearth, as he would never tire;
 The home-baked loaf, the Indian bean's perfume,
 Fill with their homely cheer the panelled room.
Come, crazy storm! And thou, wild glittering hail,
Rave o'er the roof and wave your icy veil;
Shout in our ears and take your madcap way!
I laugh at storms! for Roderick comes to-day.

The Lark's Song

The morning is wild and dark,
 The night mist runs on the vale,
Bright Lucifer dies to a spark,
 And the wind whistles up for a gale.
And stormy the day may be
 That breaks through its prison bars,
But it brings no regret to me,
 For I sing at the door of the stars!

Along the dim ocean-verge
 I see the ships labouring on;
They rise on the lifting surge
 One moment, and they are gone.
I see on the twilight plain
 The flash of the flying cars;
Men travail in joy or pain --
 But I sing at the door of the stars!

I see the green, sleeping world,
 The pastures all glazed with rime;
The smoke from the chimney curled;
 I hear the faint church bells chime.
I see the grey mountain crest,
 The slopes, and the forest spars,
With the dying moon on their breast --
 While I sing at the door of the stars!

Edward Booth Loughran.

Dead Leaves

When these dead leaves were green, love,
 November's skies were blue,
And summer came with lips aflame,
 The gentle spring to woo;
And to us, wandering hand in hand,
 Life was a fairy scene,
That golden morning in the woods
 When these dead leaves were green!

How dream-like now that dewy morn,
 Sweet with the wattle's flowers,
When love, love, love was all our theme,
 And youth and hope were ours!
Two happier hearts in all the land
 There were not then, I ween,
Than those young lovers' -- yours and mine --
 When these dead leaves were green.

How gaily did you pluck these leaves
 From the acacia's bough,
To mark the lyric we had read --
 I can repeat it now!

While came the words, like music sweet,
 Your smiling lips between --
"So fold my love within your heart,"
 When these dead leaves were green!

How many springs have passed since then?
 Ah, wherefore should we count,
The years that sped, like waters fled
 From Time's unstaying fount?
We've had our share of happiness,
 Our share of care have seen;
But love alone has never flown
 Since these dead leaves were green.

Your heart is kind and loving still,
 Your face to me as fair,
As when, that morn, the sunshine played
 Amid your golden hair.
So, dearest, sweethearts still we'll be,
 As we have ever been,
And keep our love as fresh and true
 As when these leaves were green.

Isolation

Man lives alone; star-like, each soul
 In its own orbit circles ever;
Myriads may by or round it roll --
 The ways may meet, but mingle never.

Self-pois'd, each soul its course pursues
  In light or dark, companionless:
Drop into drop may blend the dews --
  The spirit's law is loneliness.

If seemingly two souls unite,
  'Tis but as joins yon silent mere
The stream that through it, flashing bright,
  Carries its waters swift and clear.

The fringes of the rushing tide
  May on the lake's calm bosom sleep --
Its hidden spirit doth abide
  Apart, still bearing toward the deep.

O Love, to me more dear than life!
  O Friend, more faithful than a brother!
How many a bitter inward strife
  Our souls have never told each other!

We journey side by side for years,
  We dream our lives, our hopes are one --
And with some chance-said word appears
  The spanless gulf, so long unknown!

For candour's want yet neither blame;
  Even to ourselves but half-confessed,
Glows in each heart some silent flame,
  Blooms some hope-violet of the breast.

And temptings dark, and struggles deep
  There are, each soul alone must bear,
Through midnight hours unblest with sleep,

Through burning noontides of despair.

And kindly is the ordinance sent
 By which each spirit dwells apart --
Could Love or Friendship live, if rent
 The "Bluebeard chambers of the heart"?

Ishmonie

The traveller tells how, in that ancient clime
Whose mystic monuments and ruins hoar
Still struggle with the antiquary's lore,
To guard the secrets of a by-gone time,
He saw, uprising from the desert bare,
Like a white ghost, a city of the dead,
With palaces and temples wondrous fair,
Where moon-horn'd Isis once was worshipped.
But silence, like a pall, did all enfold,
And the inhabitants were turn'd to stone --
Yea, stone the very heart of every one!
Once to a rich man I this tale re-told.
"Stone hearts! A traveller's myth!" -- he turn'd aside,
As Hunger begg'd, pale-featured and wild-eyed.

John Liddell Kelly.

Immortality

At twenty-five I cast my horoscope,
 And saw a future with all good things rife --
 A firm assurance of eternal life
In worlds beyond, and in this world the hope
Of deathless fame. But now my sun doth slope
 To setting, and the toil of sordid strife,
 The care of food and raiment, child and wife,
Have dimmed and narrowed all my spirit's scope.

Eternal life -- a river gulphed in sands!
 Undying fame -- a rainbow lost in clouds!
 What hope of immortality remains
But this: "Some soul that loves and understands
 Shall save thee from the darkness that enshrouds";
 And this: "Thy blood shall course in others' veins"?

Heredity

More than a fleshly immortality

Is mine. Though I myself return again
 To dust, my qualities of heart and brain,
Of soul and spirit, shall not cease to be.
I view them growing, day by day, in thee,
 My first-begotten son; I trace them plain
 In you, my daughters; and I count it gain
Myself renewed and multiplied to see.

But sadness mingles with my selfish joy,
 At thought of what you may be called to bear.
Oh, passionate maid! Oh, glad, impulsive boy!
 Your father's sad experience you must share --
Self-torture, the unfeeling world's annoy,
 Gross pleasure, fierce exultance, grim despair!

Robert Richardson.

A Ballade of Wattle Blossom

There's a land that is happy and fair,
 Set gem-like in halcyon seas;
The white winters visit not there,
 To sadden its blossoming leas,
 More bland than the Hesperides,
Or any warm isle of the West,

Where the wattle-bloom perfumes the breeze,
And the bell-bird builds her nest.

When the oak and the elm are bare,
 And wild winds vex the shuddering trees;
There the clematis whitens the air,
 And the husbandman laughs as he sees
 The grass rippling green to his knees,
And his vineyards in emerald drest --
 Where the wattle-bloom bends in the breeze,
And the bell-bird builds her nest.

What land is with this to compare?
 Not the green hills of Hybla, with bees
Honey-sweet, are more radiant and rare
 In colour and fragrance than these
 Boon shores, where the storm-clouds cease,
And the wind and the wave are at rest --
 Where the wattle-bloom waves in the breeze,
And the bell-bird builds her nest.

    Envoy.

Sweetheart, let them praise as they please
 Other lands, but we know which is best --
Where the wattle-bloom perfumes the breeze,
 And the bell-bird builds her nest.

A Song

Above us only
 The Southern stars,
And the moon o'er brimming
 Her golden bars.
And a song sweet and clear
 As the bell-bird's plaint,
Hums low in my ear
 Like a dream-echo faint.
   The kind old song --
   How did it go?
   With its ripple and flow,
   That you used to sing, dear,
   Long ago.

Hand fast in hand,
 I, love, and thou;
Hand locked in hand,
 And on my brow
Your perfumed lips
 Breathing love and life --
The love of the maiden,
 The trust of the wife.
   And I'm listening still
   To the ripple and flow --
   How did it go? --
   Of the little French song
   Of that long ago.

Can you recall it
 Across the years?
You used to sing it
 With laughter and tears.
If you sang it now, dear,
 That kind old refrain,
It would bring back the fragrance
 Of the dead years again.
   Le printemps pour l'amour --
   How did it go?
   Only we know;
   Sing it, sweetheart, to-night,
   As you did long ago.

James Lister Cuthbertson.

Australia Federata

Australia! land of lonely lake
 And serpent-haunted fen;
Land of the torrent and the fire
 And forest-sundered men:
Thou art not now as thou shalt be
 When the stern invaders come,
In the hush before the hurricane,

The dread before the drum.

A louder thunder shall be heard
 Than echoes on thy shore,
When o'er the blackened basalt cliffs
 The foreign cannon roar --
When the stand is made in the sheoaks' shade
 When heroes fall for thee,
And the creeks in gloomy gullies run
 Dark crimson to the sea:

When under honeysuckles gray,
 And wattles' swaying gold,
The stalwart arm may strike no more,
 The valiant heart is cold --
When thou shalt know the agony,
 The fever, and the strife
Of those who wrestle against odds
 For liberty and life:

Then is the great Dominion born,
 The seven sisters bound,
From Sydney's greenly wooded port
 To lone King George's Sound --
Then shall the islands of the south,
 The lands of bloom and snow,
Forth from their isolation come
 To meet the common foe.

Then, only then -- when after war
 Is peace with honour born,
When from the bosom of the night
 Comes golden-sandalled morn,

When laurelled victory is thine,
 And the day of battle done,
Shall the heart of a mighty people stir,
 And Australia be as one.

At Cape Schanck

Down to the lighthouse pillar
 The rolling woodland comes,
Gay with the gold of she-oaks
 And the green of the stunted gums,
With the silver-grey of honeysuckle,
 With the wasted bracken red,
With a tuft of softest emerald
 And a cloud-flecked sky o'erhead.

We climbed by ridge and boulder,
 Umber and yellow scarred,
Out to the utmost precipice,
 To the point that was ocean-barred,
Till we looked below on the fastness
 Of the breeding eagle's nest,
And Cape Wollomai opened eastward
 And the Otway on the west.

Over the mirror of azure
 The purple shadows crept,
League upon league of rollers
 Landward evermore swept,
And burst upon gleaming basalt,

And foamed in cranny and crack,
And mounted in sheets of silver,
And hurried reluctant back.

And the sea, so calm out yonder,
 Wherever we turned our eyes,
Like the blast of an angel's trumpet
 Rang out to the earth and skies,
Till the reefs and the rocky ramparts
 Throbbed to the giant fray,
And the gullies and jutting headlands
 Were bathed in a misty spray.

Oh, sweet in the distant ranges,
 To the ear of inland men,
Is the ripple of falling water
 In sassafras-haunted glen,
The stir in the ripening cornfield
 That gently rustles and swells,
The wind in the wattle sighing,
 The tinkle of cattle bells.

But best is the voice of ocean,
 That strikes to the heart and brain,
That lulls with its passionate music
 Trouble and grief and pain,
That murmurs the requiem sweetest
 For those who have loved and lost,
And thunders a jubilant anthem
 To brave hearts tempest-tossed.

That takes to its boundless bosom
 The burden of all our care,

That whispers of sorrow vanquished,
 Of hours that may yet be fair,
That tells of a Harbour of Refuge
 Beyond life's stormy straits,
Of an infinite peace that gladdens,
 Of an infinite love that waits.

Wattle and Myrtle

Gold of the tangled wilderness of wattle,
 Break in the lone green hollows of the hills,
Flame on the iron headlands of the ocean,
 Gleam on the margin of the hurrying rills.

Come with thy saffron diadem and scatter
 Odours of Araby that haunt the air,
Queen of our woodland, rival of the roses,
 Spring in the yellow tresses of thy hair.

Surely the old gods, dwellers on Olympus,
 Under thy shining loveliness have strayed,
Crowned with thy clusters, magical Apollo,
 Pan with his reedy music may have played.

Surely within thy fastness, Aphrodite,
 She of the sea-ways, fallen from above,
Wandered beneath thy canopy of blossom,
 Nothing disdainful of a mortal's love.

Aye, and Her sweet breath lingers on the wattle,

Aye, and Her myrtle dominates the glade,
And with a deep and perilous enchantment
 Melts in the heart of lover and of maid.

The Australian Sunrise

The Morning Star paled slowly, the Cross hung low to the sea,
And down the shadowy reaches the tide came swirling free,
The lustrous purple blackness of the soft Australian night,
Waned in the gray awakening that heralded the light;
Still in the dying darkness, still in the forest dim
The pearly dew of the dawning clung to each giant limb,
Till the sun came up from ocean, red with the cold sea mist,
And smote on the limestone ridges, and the shining tree-tops kissed;
Then the fiery Scorpion vanished, the magpie's note was heard,
And the wind in the she-oak wavered, and the honeysuckles stirred,
The airy golden vapour rose from the river breast,
The kingfisher came darting out of his crannied nest,
And the bulrushes and reed-beds put off their sallow gray
And burnt with cloudy crimson at dawning of the day.

John Farrell.

Australia to England

June 22nd, 1897

What of the years of Englishmen?
 What have they brought of growth and grace
Since mud-built London by its fen
 Became the Briton's breeding-place?
What of the Village, where our blood
 Was brewed by sires, half man, half brute,
In vessels of wild womanhood,
 From blood of Saxon, Celt and Jute?

What are its gifts, this Harvest Home
 Of English tilth and English cost,
Where fell the hamlet won by Rome
 And rose the city that she lost?
O! terrible and grand and strange
 Beyond all phantasy that gleams
When Hope, asleep, sees radiant Change
 Come to her through the halls of dreams!

A heaving sea of life, that beats
 Like England's heart of pride to-day,
And up from roaring miles of streets

Flings on the roofs its human spray;
And fluttering miles of flags aflow,
 And cannon's voice, and boom of bell,
And seas of fire to-night, as though
 A hundred cities flamed and fell;

While, under many a fair festoon
 And flowering crescent, set ablaze
With all the dyes that English June
 Can lend to deck a day of days,
And past where mart and palace rise,
 And shrine and temple lift their spears,
Below five million misted eyes
 Goes a grey Queen of Sixty Years --

Go lords, and servants of the lords
 Of earth, with homage on their lips,
And kinsmen carrying English swords,
 And offering England battle-ships;
And tribute-payers, on whose hands
 Their English fetters scarce appear;
And gathered round from utmost lands
 Ambassadors of Love and Fear!

Dim signs of greeting waved afar,
 Far trumpets blown and flags unfurled,
And England's name an Avatar
 Of light and sound throughout the world --
Hailed Empress among nations, Queen
 Enthroned in solemn majesty,
On splendid proofs of what has been,
 And presages of what will be!

For this your sons, foreseeing not
  Or heeding not, the aftermath,
Because their strenuous hearts were hot
  Went first on many a cruel path,
And, trusting first and last to blows,
  Fed death with such as would gainsay
Their instant passing, or oppose
  With talk of Right strength's right of way!

For this their names are on the stone
  Of mountain spires, and carven trees
That stand in flickering wastes unknown
  Wait with their dying messages;
When fire blasts dance with desert drifts
  The English bones show white below,
And, not so white, when summer lifts
  The counterpane of Yukon's snow.

Condemned by blood to reach for grapes
  That hang in sight, however high,
Beyond the smoke of Asian capes,
  The nameless, dauntless, dead ones lie;
And where Sierran morning shines
  On summits rolling out like waves,
By many a brow of royal pines
  The noisiest find quiet graves.

By lust of flesh and lust of gold,
  And depth of loins and hairy breadth
Of breast, and hands to take and hold,
  And boastful scorn of pain and death,
And something more of manliness
  Than tamer men, and growing shame

Of shameful things, and something less
 Of final faith in sword and flame --

By many a battle fought for wrong,
 And many a battle fought for right,
So have you grown august and strong,
 Magnificent in all men's sight --
A voice for which the kings have ears,
 A face the craftiest statesmen scan;
A mind to mould the after years,
 And mint the destinies of man!

Red sins were yours: the avid greed
 Of pirate fathers, smocked as Grace,
Sent Judas missioners to read
 Christ's Word to many a feebler race --
False priests of Truth who made their tryst
 At Mammon's shrine, and reft or slew --
Some hands you taught to pray to Christ
 Have prayed His curse to rest on you!

Your way has been to pluck the blade
 Too readily, and train the guns.
We here, apart and unafraid
 Of envious foes, are but your sons:
We stretched a heedless hand to smutch
 Our spotless flag with Murder's blight --
For one less sacrilegious touch
 God's vengeance blasted Uzza white!

You vaunted most of forts and fleets,
 And courage proved in battle-feasts,
The courage of the beast that eats

His torn and quivering fellow-beasts;
Your pride of deadliest armament --
What is it but the self-same dint
Of joy with which the Caveman bent
To shape a bloodier axe of flint?

But praise to you, and more than praise
And thankfulness, for some things done;
And blessedness, and length of days
As long as earth shall last, or sun!
You first among the peoples spoke
Sharp words and angry questionings
Which burst the bonds and shed the yoke
That made your men the slaves of Kings!

You set and showed the whole world's school
The lesson it will surely read,
That each one ruled has right to rule --
The alphabet of Freedom's creed
Which slowly wins it proselytes
And makes uneasier many a throne;
You taught them all to prate of Rights
In language growing like your own!

And now your holiest and best
And wisest dream of such a tie
As, holding hearts from East to West,
Shall strengthen while the years go by:
And of a time when every man
For every fellow-man will do
His kindliest, working by the plan
God set him. May the dream come true!

And greater dreams! O Englishmen,
  Be sure the safest time of all
For even the mightiest State is when
  Not even the least desires its fall!
Make England stand supreme for aye,
  Because supreme for peace and good,
Warned well by wrecks of yesterday
  That strongest feet may slip in blood!

Arthur Patchett Martin.

Bushland

Not sweeter to the storm-tossed mariner
  Is glimpse of home, where wife and children wait
  To welcome him with kisses at the gate,
Than to the town-worn man the breezy stir
  Of mountain winds on rugged pathless heights:
  His long-pent soul drinks in the deep delights
That Nature hath in store. The sun-kissed bay
  Gleams thro' the grand old gnarled gum-tree boughs
Like burnished brass; the strong-winged bird of prey
Sweeps by, upon his lonely vengeful way --
  While over all, like breath of holy vows,
  The sweet airs blow, and the high-vaulted sky

Looks down in pity this fair Summer day
 On all poor earth-born creatures doomed to die.

Douglas Brooke Wheelton Sladen.

Under the Wattle

"Why should not wattle do
 For mistletoe?"
Asked one -- they were but two --
 Where wattles grow.

He was her lover, too,
 Who urged her so --
"Why should not wattle do
 For mistletoe?"

A rose-cheek rosier grew;
 Rose-lips breathed low;
"Since it is here, and YOU,
 I hardly know
Why wattle should not do."

Victor James Daley.

Players

And after all -- and after all,
 Our passionate prayers, and sighs, and tears,
Is life a reckless carnival?
 And are they lost, our golden years?

Ah, no; ah, no; for, long ago,
 Ere time could sear, or care could fret,
There was a youth called Romeo,
 There was a maid named Juliet.

The players of the past are gone;
 The races rise; the races pass;
And softly over all is drawn
 The quiet Curtain of the Grass.

But when the world went wild with Spring,
 What days we had! Do you forget?
When I of all the world was King,
 And you were my Queen Juliet?

The things that are; the things that seem --
 Who shall distinguish shape from show?

The great processional, splendid dream
  Of life is all I wish to know.

The gods their faces turn away
  From nations and their little wars;
But we our golden drama play
  Before the footlights of the stars.

There lives -- though Time should cease to flow,
  And stars their courses should forget --
There lives a grey-haired Romeo,
  Who loves a golden Juliet.

Anna

The pale discrowned stacks of maize,
  Like spectres in the sun,
Stand shivering nigh Avonaise,
  Where all is dead and gone.

The sere leaves make a music vain,
  With melancholy chords;
Like cries from some old battle-plain,
  Like clash of phantom swords.

But when the maize was lush and green
  With musical green waves,
She went, its plumed ranks between,
  Unto the hill of graves.

There you may see sweet flowers set
 O'er damsels and o'er dames --
Rose, Ellen, Mary, Margaret --
 The sweet old quiet names.

The gravestones show in long array,
 Though white or green with moss,
How linked in Life and Death are they --
 The Shamrock and the Cross.

The gravestones face the Golden East,
 And in the morn they take
The blessing of the Great High Priest,
 Before the living wake.

Who was she? Never ask her name,
 Her beauty and her grace
Have passed, with her poor little shame,
 Into the Silent Place.

In Avonaise, in Avonaise,
 Where all is dead and done,
The folk who rest there all their days
 Care not for moon or sun.

They care not, when the living pass,
 Whether they sigh or smile;
They hear above their graves the grass
 That sighs -- "A little while!"

A white stone marks her small green bed
 With "Anna" and "Adieu".
Madonna Mary, rest her head

On your dear lap of blue!

The Night Ride

The red sun on the lonely lands
  Gazed, under clouds of rose,
As one who under knitted hands
  Takes one last look and goes.

Then Pain, with her white sister Fear,
  Crept nearer to my bed:
"The sands are running; dost thou hear
  Thy sobbing heart?" she said.

There came a rider to the gate,
  And stern and clear spake he:
"For meat or drink thou must not wait,
  But rise and ride with me."

I waited not for meat or drink,
  Or kiss, or farewell kind --
But oh! my heart was sore to think
  Of friends I left behind.

We rode o'er hills that seemed to sweep
  Skyward like swelling waves;
The living stirred not in their sleep,
  The dead slept in their graves.

And ever as we rode I heard

A moan of anguish sore --
No voice of man or beast or bird,
 But all of these and more.

"Is it the moaning of the Earth?
 Dark Rider, answer me!"
"It is the cry of life at birth"
 He answered quietly:

"But thou canst turn a face of cheer
 To good days still in store;
Thou needst not care for Pain or Fear --
 They cannot harm thee more."

Yet I rode on with sullen heart,
 And said with breaking breath,
"If thou art he I think thou art,
 Then slay me now, O Death!"

The veil was from my eyesight drawn --
 "Thou knowest now," said he:
"I am the Angel of the Dawn!
 Ride back, and wait for me."

So I rode back at morning light,
 And there, beside my bed,
Fear had become a lily white
 And Pain a rose of red.

Alice Werner.

Bannerman of the Dandenong

I rode through the Bush in the burning noon,
 Over the hills to my bride, --
The track was rough and the way was long,
And Bannerman of the Dandenong,
 He rode along by my side.

A day's march off my Beautiful dwelt,
 By the Murray streams in the West; --
Lightly lilting a gay love-song
Rode Bannerman of the Dandenong,
 With a blood-red rose on his breast.

"Red, red rose of the Western streams"
 Was the song he sang that day --
Truest comrade in hour of need, --
Bay Mathinna his peerless steed --
 I had my own good grey.

There fell a spark on the upland grass --
 The dry Bush leapt into flame; --
And I felt my heart go cold as death,
And Bannerman smiled and caught his breath, --

But I heard him name Her name.

Down the hill-side the fire-floods rushed,
 On the roaring eastern wind; --
Neck and neck was the reckless race, --
Ever the bay mare kept her pace,
 But the grey horse dropped behind.

He turned in the saddle -- "Let's change, I say!"
 And his bridle rein he drew.
He sprang to the ground, -- "Look sharp!" he said
With a backward toss of his curly head --
 "I ride lighter than you!"

Down and up -- it was quickly done --
 No words to waste that day! --
Swift as a swallow she sped along,
The good bay mare from Dandenong, --
 And Bannerman rode the grey.

The hot air scorched like a furnace blast
 From the very mouth of Hell: --
The blue gums caught and blazed on high
Like flaming pillars into the sky; . . .
 The grey horse staggered and fell.

"Ride, ride, lad, -- ride for her sake!" he cried; --
 Into the gulf of flame
Were swept, in less than a breathing space
The laughing eyes, and the comely face,
 And the lips that named HER name.

She bore me bravely, the good bay mare; --

Stunned, and dizzy and blind,
I heard the sound of a mingling roar --
'Twas the Lachlan River that rushed before,
And the flames that rolled behind.

Safe -- safe, at Nammoora gate,
 I fell, and lay like a stone.
O love! thine arms were about me then,
Thy warm tears called me to life again, --
 But -- O God! that I came alone! --

We dwell in peace, my beautiful one
 And I, by the streams in the West, --
But oft through the mist of my dreams along
Rides Bannerman of the Dandenong,
 With the blood-red rose on his breast.

Ethel Castilla.

An Australian Girl

"She's pretty to walk with,
And witty to talk with,
And pleasant, too, to think on."
    Sir John Suckling.

She has a beauty of her own,
A beauty of a paler tone
   Than English belles;
Yet southern sun and southern air
Have kissed her cheeks, until they wear
The dainty tints that oft appear
   On rosy shells.

Her frank, clear eyes bespeak a mind
Old-world traditions fail to bind.
   She is not shy
Or bold, but simply self-possessed;
Her independence adds a zest
Unto her speech, her piquant jest,
   Her quaint reply.

O'er classic volumes she will pore
With joy; and true scholastic lore
   Will often gain.
In sports she bears away the bell,
Nor, under music's siren spell,
To dance divinely, flirt as well,
   Does she disdain.

A Song of Sydney

(1894)

High headlands all jealously hide thee,

O fairest of sea-girdled towns!
Thine Ocean-spouse smileth beside thee,
  While each headland threatens and frowns.
Like Venice, upheld on sea-pinion,
  And fated to reign o'er the free,
Thou wearest, in sign of dominion,
    The zone of the sea.

No winter thy fertile slope hardens,
  O new Florence, set in the South!
All lands give their flowers to thy gardens,
  That glow to thy bright harbour's mouth;
The waratah and England's red roses
  With stately magnolias entwine,
Gay sunflowers fill sea-scented closes,
    All sweet with woodbine.

Thy harbour's fair flower-crowned islands
  See flags of all countries unfurled,
Thou smilest from green, sunlit highlands
  To open thine arms to the world!
Dark East's and fair West's emulations
  Resound from each hill-shadowed quay,
And over the songs of all nations,
    The voice of the sea.

Francis William Lauderdale Adams.

Something

It is something in this darker dream demented
 to have wrestled with its pleasure and its pain:
it is something to have sinned, and have repented:
 it is something to have failed, and tried again!

It is something to have loved the brightest Beauty
 with no hope of aught but silence for your vow:
it is something to have tried to do your duty:
 it is something to be trying, trying now!

And, in the silent solemn hours,
 when your soul floats down the far faint flood of time --
to think of Earth's lovers who are ours,
 of her saviours saving, suffering, sublime:

And that you with THESE may be her lover,
 with THESE may save and suffer for her sake --
IT IS JOY TO HAVE LIVED, SO TO DISCOVER
 YOU'VE A LIFE YOU CAN GIVE AND SHE CAN TAKE!

Gordon's Grave

All the heat and the glow and the hush
 of the summer afternoon;
the scent of the sweet-briar bush
 over bowing grass-blades and broom;

the birds that flit and pass;
 singing the song he knows,
the grass-hopper in the grass;
 the voice of the she-oak boughs.

Ah, and the shattered column
 crowned with the poet's wreath.
Who, who keeps silent and solemn
 his passing place beneath?

~This was a poet that loved God's breath;
 his life was a passionate quest;
he looked down deep in the wells of death,
 and now he is taking his rest.~

To A. L. Gordon

In night-long days, in aeons
 where all Time's nights are one;
where life and death sing paeans

as of Greeks and Galileans,
 never begun or done;

where fate, the slow swooping condor,
 comes glooming all the sky --
as you have pondered I ponder,
as you have wandered I wander,
 as you have died, shall I die?

Love and Death

Death? is it death you give? So be it! O Death,
 thou hast been long my friend, and now thy pale
cool cheek shall have my kiss, while the faint breath
expires on thy still lips, O lovely Death!

Come then, loose hands, fair Life, without a wail!
 We've had good hours together, and you were sweet
what time love whispered with the nightingale,
tho' ever your music by the lark's would fail.

Come then, loose hands! Our lover time is done.
Now is the marriage with the eternal sun.
 The hours are few that rest, are few and fleet.
Good-bye! The game is lost: the game is won.

Thomas William Heney.

Absence

Ah, happy air that, rough or soft,
  May kiss that face and stay;
And happy beams that from above
  May choose to her their way;
And happy flowers that now and then
  Touch lips more sweet than they!

But it were not so blest to be
  Or light or air or rose;
Those dainty fingers tear and toss
  The bloom that in them glows;
And come or go, both wind and ray
  She heeds not, if she knows.

But if I come thy choice should be
  Either to love or not --
For if I might I would not kiss
  And then be all forgot;
And it were best thy love to lose
  If love self-scorn begot.

A Riverina Road

Now while so many turn with love and longing
 To wan lands lying in the grey North Sea,
To thee we turn, hearts, mem'ries, all belonging,
 Dear land of ours, to thee.

West, ever west, with the strong sunshine marching
 Beyond the mountains, far from this soft coast,
Until we almost see the great plains arching,
 In endless mirage lost.

A land of camps where seldom is sojourning,
 Where men like the dim fathers of our race,
Halt for a time, and next day, unreturning,
 Fare ever on apace.

Last night how many a leaping blaze affrighted
 The wailing birds of passage in their file;
And dawn sees ashes dead and embers whited
 Where men had dwelt awhile.

The sun may burn, the mirage shift and vanish
 And fade and glare by turns along the sky;
The haze of heat may all the distance banish
 To the uncaring eye.

By speech, or tongue of bird or brute, unbroken
 Silence may brood upon the lifeless plain,
Nor any sign, far off or near, betoken

Man in this vast domain.

Though tender grace the landscape lacks, too spacious,
 Impassive, silent, lonely, to be fair,
Their kindness swiftly comes more soft and gracious,
 Who live or tarry there.

All that he has, in camp or homestead, proffers
 To stranger guest at once a stranger host,
Proudest to see accepted what he offers,
 Given without a boast.

Pass, if you can, the drover's cattle stringing
 Along the miles of the wide travelled road,
Without a challenge through the hot dust ringing,
 Kind though abrupt the mode.

A cloud of dust where polish'd wheels are flashing
 Passes along, and in it rolls the mail.
Comes from the box as on the coach goes dashing
 The lonely driver's hail.

Or in the track a station youngster mounted
 Sits in his saddle smoking for a "spell",
Rides a while onward; then, his news recounted,
 Parts with a brief farewell.

To-day these plains may seem a face defiant,
 Turn'd to a mortal foe, yet scorning fear;
As when, with heaven at war, an Earth-born giant
 Saw the Olympian near.

Come yet again! No child's fair face is sweeter

With young delight than this cool blooming land,
Silent no more, for songs than wings are fleeter,
 No blaze, but sunshine bland.

Thus in her likeness that strange nature moulding
 Makes man as moody, sad and savage too;
Yet in his heart, like her, a passion holding,
 Unselfish, kind and true.

Therefore, while many turn with love and longing
 To wan lands lying on the grey North Sea,
To-day possessed by other mem'ries thronging
 We turn, wild West, to thee!

23rd December, 1891.

Patrick Edward Quinn.

A Girl's Grave

"Aged 17, OF A BROKEN HEART, January 1st, 1841."

What story is here of broken love,
 What idyllic sad romance,
What arrow fretted the silken dove

That met with such grim mischance?

I picture you, sleeper of long ago,
  When you trifled and danced and smiled,
All golden laughter and beauty's glow
  In a girl life sweet and wild.

Hair with the red gold's luring tinge,
  Fine as the finest silk,
Violet eyes with a golden fringe
  And cheeks of roses and milk.

Something of this you must have been,
  Something gentle and sweet,
To have broken your heart at seventeen
  And died in such sad defeat.

Hardly one of your kinsfolk live,
  It was all so long ago,
The tale of the cruel love to give
  That laid you here so low.

Loving, trusting, and foully paid --
  The story is easily guessed,
A blotted sun and skies that fade
  And this grass-grown grave the rest.

Whatever the cynic may sourly say,
  With a dash of truth, I ween,
Of the girls of the period, in your day
  They had hearts at seventeen.

Dead of a fashion out of date,

Such folly has passed away
Like the hoop and patch and modish gait
　That went out with an older day.

The stone is battered and all awry,
　The words can be scarcely read,
The rank reeds clustering thick and high
　Over your buried head.

I pluck one straight as a Paynim's lance
　To keep your memory green,
For the lordly sake of old Romance
　And your own, sad seventeen.

John Sandes.

`With Death's Prophetic Ear'

Lay my rifle here beside me, set my Bible on my breast,
　For a moment let the warning bugles cease;
As the century is closing I am going to my rest,
　Lord, lettest Thou Thy servant go in peace.
But loud through all the bugles rings a cadence in mine ear,
　And on the winds my hopes of peace are strowed.
Those winds that waft the voices that already I can hear
　Of the rooi-baatjes singing on the road.

Yes, the red-coats are returning, I can hear the steady tramp,
  After twenty years of waiting, lulled to sleep,
Since rank and file at Potchefstroom we hemmed them in their camp,
  And cut them up at Bronkerspruit like sheep.
They shelled us at Ingogo, but we galloped into range,
  And we shot the British gunners where they showed.
I guessed they would return to us, I knew the chance must change --
  Hark! the rooi-baatjes singing on the road!

But now from snow-swept Canada, from India's torrid plains,
  From lone Australian outposts, hither led,
Obeying their commando, as they heard the bugle's strains,
  The men in brown have joined the men in red.
They come to find the colours at Majuba left and lost,
  They come to pay us back the debt they owed;
And I hear new voices lifted, and I see strange colours tossed,
  'Mid the rooi-baatjes singing on the road.

The old, old faiths must falter, and the old, old creeds must fail --
  I hear it in that distant murmur low --
The old, old order changes, and 'tis vain for us to rail,
  The great world does not want us -- we must go.
And veldt, and spruit, and kopje to the stranger will belong,
  No more to trek before him we shall load;
Too well, too well, I know it, for I hear it in the song
  Of the rooi-baatjes singing on the road.

Inez K. Hyland.

To a Wave

Where were you yesterday? In Gulistan,
 With roses and the frenzied nightingales?
Rather would I believe you shining ran
 With peaceful floods, where the soft voice prevails
Of building doves in lordly trees set high,
 Trees which enclose a home where love abides --
His love and hers, a passioned ecstasy;
 Your tone has caught its echo and derides
My joyless lot, as face down pressed I lie
 Upon the shifting sand, and hear the reeds
Voicing a thin, dissonant threnody
 Unto the cliff and wind-tormented weeds.
As with the faint half-lights of jade toward
 The shore you come and show a violet hue,
I wonder if the face of my adored
 Was ever held importraitured by you.
Ah, no! if you had seen his face, still prest
 Within your hold the picture dear would be,
Like that bright portrait which so moved the breast
 Of fairest Gurd with soft unrest that she,
Born in ice halls, she who but raised her eyes
 And scornful questioned, "What is love, indeed?

None ever viewed it 'neath these northern skies," --
  Seeing the face soon learned love's gentle creed;
But you hold nothing to be counted dear --
  Only a gift of weed and broken shells;
Yet I will gather one, so I can hear
  The soft remembrance which still in it dwells:
For in the shell, though broken, ever lies
  The murmur of the sea whence it was torn --
So in a woman's heart there never dies
  The memory of love, though love be lorn.

Bread and Wine

A cup of opal
  Through which there glows
The cream of the pearl,
  The heart of the rose;
And the blue of the sea
  Where Australia lies,
And the amber flush
  Of her sunset skies,
And the emerald tints
  Of the dragon fly
Shall stain my cup
  With their brilliant dye.
And into this cup
  I would pour the wine
Of youth and health
  And the gifts divine
Of music and song,

And the sweet content
Which must ever belong
 To a life well spent.
And what bread would I break
 With my wine, think you?
The bread of a love
 That is pure and true.

George Essex Evans.

An Australian Symphony

Not as the songs of other lands
   Her song shall be
Where dim Her purple shore-line stands
   Above the sea!
As erst she stood, she stands alone;
Her inspiration is her own.
From sunlit plains to mangrove strands
Not as the songs of other lands
   Her song shall be.

O Southern Singers! Rich and sweet,
   Like chimes of bells,
The cadence swings with rhythmic beat

    The music swells;
But undertones, weird, mournful, strong,
Sweep like swift currents thro' the song.
In deepest chords, with passion fraught,
In softest notes of sweetest thought,
   This sadness dwells.

Is this her song, so weirdly strange,
   So mixed with pain,
That whereso'er her poets range
   Is heard the strain?
Broods there no spell upon the air
But desolation and despair?
No voice, save Sorrow's, to intrude
Upon her mountain solitude
   Or sun-kissed plain?

The silence and the sunshine creep
   With soft caress
O'er billowy plain and mountain steep
   And wilderness --
A velvet touch, a subtle breath,
As sweet as love, as calm as death,
On earth, on air, so soft, so fine,
Till all the soul a spell divine
   O'ershadoweth.

The gray gums by the lonely creek,
   The star-crowned height,
The wind-swept plain, the dim blue peak,
   The cold white light,
The solitude spread near and far
Around the camp-fire's tiny star,

The horse-bell's melody remote,
The curlew's melancholy note
  Across the night.

These have their message; yet from these
  Our songs have thrown
O'er all our Austral hills and leas
  One sombre tone.
Whence doth the mournful keynote start?
From the pure depths of Nature's heart?
Or from the heart of him who sings
And deems his hand upon the strings
  Is Nature's own?

Could tints be deeper, skies less dim,
  More soft and fair,
Dappled with milk-white clouds that swim
  In faintest air?
The soft moss sleeps upon the stone,
Green scrub-vine traceries enthrone
The dead gray trunks, and boulders red,
Roofed by the pine and carpeted
  With maidenhair.

But far and near, o'er each, o'er all,
  Above, below,
Hangs the great silence like a pall
  Softer than snow.
Not sorrow is the spell it brings,
But thoughts of calmer, purer things,
Like the sweet touch of hands we love,
A woman's tenderness above
  A fevered brow.

These purple hills, these yellow leas,
   These forests lone,
These mangrove shores, these shimmering seas,
   This summer zone --
Shall they inspire no nobler strain
Than songs of bitterness and pain?
Strike her wild harp with firmer hand,
And send her music thro' the land,
   With loftier tone!

    . . . . .

Her song is silence; unto her
   Its mystery clings.
Silence is the interpreter
   Of deeper things.
O for sonorous voice and strong
To change that silence into song,
To give that melody release
Which sleeps in the deep heart of peace
   With folded wings!

A Nocturne

Like weary sea-birds spent with flight
   And faltering,
The slow hours beat across the night
   On leaden wing.
The wild bird knows where rest shall be

Soe'er he roam.
Heart of my heart! apart from thee
  I have no home.

Afar from thee, yet not alone,
  Heart of my heart!
Like some soft haunting whisper blown
  From Heaven thou art.
I hear the magic music roll
  Its waves divine;
The subtle fragrance of thy soul
  Has passed to mine.

Nor dawn nor Heaven my heart can know
  Save that which lies
In lights and shades that come and go
  In thy soft eyes.
Here in the night I dream the day,
  By love upborne,
When thy sweet eyes shall shine and say
  "It is the morn!"

A Pastoral

Nature feels the touch of noon;
 Not a rustle stirs the grass;
Not a shadow flecks the sky,
Save the brown hawk hovering nigh;
 Not a ripple dims the glass
    Of the wide lagoon.

Darkly, like an armed host
 Seen afar against the blue,
Rise the hills, and yellow-grey
Sleeps the plain in cove and bay,
 Like a shining sea that dreams
   Round a silent coast.

From the heart of these blue hills,
 Like the joy that flows from peace,
Creeps the river far below
Fringed with willow, sinuous, slow.
 Surely here there seems surcease
   From the care that kills.

Surely here might radiant Love
 Fill with happiness his cup,
Where the purple lucerne-bloom
Floods the air with sweet perfume,
 Nature's incense floating up
   To the Gods above.

'Neath the gnarled-boughed apple trees
 Motionless the cattle stand;
Chequered cornfield, homestead white,
Sleeping in the streaming light,
 For deep trance is o'er the land,
   And the wings of peace.

Here, O Power that moves the heart,
 Thou art in the quiet air;
Here, unvexed of code or creed,
Man may breathe his bitter need;

Nor with impious lips declare
  What Thou wert and art.

All the strong souls of the race
 Thro' the aeons that have run,
They have cried aloud to Thee --
"Thou art that which stirs in me!"
 As the flame leaps towards the sun
  They have sought Thy face.

But the faiths have flowered and flown,
 And the truth is but in part;
Many a creed and many a grade
For Thy purpose Thou hast made.
 None can know Thee what Thou art,
  Fathomless! Unknown!

The Women of the West

They left the vine-wreathed cottage and the mansion on the hill,
The houses in the busy streets where life is never still,
The pleasures of the city, and the friends they cherished best:
For love they faced the wilderness -- the Women of the West.

The roar, and rush, and fever of the city died away,
And the old-time joys and faces -- they were gone for many a day;
In their place the lurching coach-wheel, or the creaking bullock chains,
O'er the everlasting sameness of the never-ending plains.

In the slab-built, zinc-roofed homestead of some lately taken run,

In the tent beside the bankment of a railway just begun,
In the huts on new selections, in the camps of man's unrest,
On the frontiers of the Nation, live the Women of the West.

The red sun robs their beauty, and, in weariness and pain,
The slow years steal the nameless grace that never comes again;
And there are hours men cannot soothe, and words men cannot say --
The nearest woman's face may be a hundred miles away.

The wide bush holds the secrets of their longing and desires,
When the white stars in reverence light their holy altar fires,
And silence, like the touch of God, sinks deep into the breast --
Perchance He hears and understands the Women of the West.

For them no trumpet sounds the call, no poet plies his arts --
They only hear the beating of their gallant, loving hearts.
But they have sung with silent lives the song all songs above --
The holiness of sacrifice, the dignity of love.

Well have we held our father's creed. No call has passed us by.
We faced and fought the wilderness, we sent our sons to die.
And we have hearts to do and dare, and yet, o'er all the rest,
The hearts that made the Nation were the Women of the West.

Mary Colborne-Veel.

'What Look hath She?'

What look hath she,
 What majestie,
That must so high approve her?
 What graces move
 That I so love,
That I so greatly love her?

 No majestie
 But Truth hath She;
Thoughts sweet and gracious move her;
 That straight approve
 My heart to love,
And all my life to love her!

Saturday Night

Saturday night in the crowded town;
Pleasure and pain going up and down,

Murmuring low on the ear there beat
Echoes unceasing of voice and feet.
Withered age, with its load of care,
Come in this tumult of life to share,
Childhood glad in its radiance brief,
Happiest-hearted or bowed with grief,
Meet alike, as the stars look down
Week by week on the crowded town.

~And in a kingdom of mystery,
Rapt from this weariful world to see
Magic sights in the yellow glare,
Breathing delight in the gas-lit air,
Careless of sorrow, of grief or pain,
Two by two, again and again,
Strephon and Chloe together move,
Walking in Arcady, land of love.~

What are the meanings that burden all
These murmuring voices that rise and fall?
Tragedies whispered of, secrets told,
Over the baskets of bought and sold;
Joyous speech of the lately wed;
Broken lamentings that name the dead:
Endless runes of the gossip's rede,
And gathered home with the weekly need,
Kindly greetings as neighbours meet
There in the stir of the busy street.

Then is the glare of the gaslight ray
Gifted with potency strange to-day,
Records of time-written history
Flash into sight as each face goes by.

There, as the hundreds slow moving go,
Each with his burden of joy or woe,
Souls, in the meeting of stranger's eyes,
Startled this kinship to recognise, --
Meet and part, as the stars look down,
Week by week on the crowded town.

~And still, in the midst of the busy hum,
Rapt in their dream of delight they come.
Heedless of sorrow, of grief or care,
Wandering on in enchanted air,
Far from the haunting shadow of pain:
Two by two, again and again,
Strephon and Chloe together move,
Walking in Arcady, land of love.~

`Resurgam'

(Autumn Song)

Chill breezes moaning are
  Where leaves hang yellow:
O'er the grey hills afar
  Flies the last swallow;
To come again, my love, to come again
  Blithe with the summer.
But Ah! the long months ere we welcome then
  That bright new comer.

Cold lie the flowers and dead
  Where leaves are falling.
Meekly they bowed and sped
  At Autumn's calling.
To come again, my love, to come again
  Blithe with the swallow.
Ah! might I dreaming lie at rest till then,
  Or rise and follow!

The summer blooms are gone,
  And bright birds darting;
Cold lies the earth forlorn;
  And we are parting.
To meet again, my love, to meet again
  In deathless greeting,
But ah! what wintry bitterness of pain
  Ere that far meeting!

Distant Authors

"Aqui esta encerrada el alma licenciado Pedro Garcias."

Dear books! and each the living soul,
  Our hearts aver, of men unseen,
Whose power to strengthen, charm, control,
  Surmounts all earth's green miles between.

For us at least the artists show
  Apart from fret of work-day jars:
We know them but as friends may know,

Or they are known beyond the stars.

Their mirth, their grief, their soul's desire,
 When twilight murmuring of streams,
Or skies far touched by sunset fire,
 Exalt them to pure worlds of dreams;

Their love of good; their rage at wrong;
 Their hours when struggling thought makes way;
Their hours when fancy drifts to song
 Lightly and glad as bird-trills may;

All these are truths. And if as true
 More graceless scrutiny that reads,
"These fruits amid strange husking grew;"
 "These lilies blossomed amongst weeds;"

Here no despoiling doubts shall blow,
 No fret of feud, of work-day jars.
We know them but as friends may know,
 Or they are known beyond the stars.

John Bernard O'Hara.

Happy Creek

The little creek goes winding
 Thro' gums of white and blue,
    A silver arm
    Around the farm
 It flings, a lover true;
And softly, where the rushes lean,
 It sings (O sweet and low)
    A lover's song,
    And winds along,
 How happy -- lovers know!

The little creek goes singing
 By maidenhair and moss,
    Along its banks
    In rosy ranks
 The wild flowers wave and toss;
And ever where the ferns dip down
 It sings (O sweet and low)
    A lover's song,
    And winds along,
 How happy -- lovers know!

The little creek takes colour,

From summer skies above;
  Now blue, now gold,
  Its waters fold
The clouds in closest love;
But loudly when the thunders roll
It sings (nor sweet, nor low)
  No lover's song,
  But sweeps along,
How angry -- lovers know!

The little creek for ever
Goes winding, winding down,
  Away, away,
  By night, by day,
Where dark the ranges frown;
But ever as it glides it sings,
It sings (O sweet and low)
  A lover's song,
  And winds along,
How happy -- lovers know!

A Country Village

Among the folding hills
 It lies, a quiet nook,
Where dreaming nature fills
 Sweet pages of her book,
While through the meadow flowers
She sings in summer hours,
Or weds the woodland rills

Low-laughing to the brook.

The graveyard whitely gleams
　Across the soundless vale,
So sad, so sweet, yet seems
　A watcher cold and pale
That waits through many springs
The tribute old Time brings,
And knows, though life be loud,
　The reaper may not fail.

Here come not feet of change
　From year to fading year;
Ringed by the rolling range
　No world-wide notes men hear.
The wheels of time may stand
Here in a lonely land,
Age after age may pass
　Untouched of change or cheer;

As still the farmer keeps
　The same dull round of things;
He reaps and sows and reaps,
　And clings, as ivy clings,
To old-time trust, nor cares
What science does or dares,
What lever moves the world,
　What progress spreads its wings.

Yet here, of woman born,
　Are lives that know not rest,
With fierce desires that scorn
　The quiet life as best;

That see in wider ways
Life's richer splendours blaze,
And feel ambition's fire
 Burn in their ardent breast.

Yea, some that fain would know
 Life's purpose strange and vast,
How wide is human woe,
 What wailing of the past
Still strikes the present dumb,
What phantoms go and come
Of wrongs that cry aloud,
 "At last, O God! at last!"

Here, too, are dreams that wing
 Rich regions of Romance;
Love waking when the Spring
 Begins its first wild dance,
Love redder than the rose,
Love paler than the snows,
Love frail as corn that tilts
 With morning winds a lance.

For never land so lone
 That love could find not wings
In every wind that's blown
 By lips of jewelled springs,
For love is life's sweet pain,
And when sweet life is slain
It finds a radiant rest
 Beyond the change of things.

Beyond the shocks that jar,

The chance of changing fate,
   Where fraud and violence are,
   And heedless lust and hate;
   Yet still where faith is clear,
   And honour held most dear,
   And hope that seeks the dawn
   Looks up with heart elate.

Flinders

   He left his island home
   For leagues of sleepless foam,
    For stress of alien seas,
     Where wild winds ever blow;
   For England's sake he sought
   Fresh fields of fame, and fought
    A stormy world for these
     A hundred years ago.

   And where the Austral shore
   Heard southward far the roar
    Of rising tides that came
     From lands of ice and snow,
   Beneath a gracious sky
   To fadeless memory
    He left a deathless name
     A hundred years ago.

   Yea, left a name sublime
   From that wild dawn of Time,

Whose light he haply saw
 In supreme sunrise flow,
And from the shadows vast,
That filled the dim dead past,
 A brighter glory draw,
  A hundred years ago.

Perchance, he saw in dreams
Beside our sunlit streams
 In some majestic hour
  Old England's banners blow;
Mayhap, the radiant morn
Of this great nation born,
 August with perfect power,
  A hundred years ago.

We know not, -- yet for thee
Far may the season be,
 Whose harp in shameful sleep
  Is soundless lying low!
Far be the noteless hour
That holds of fame no flower
 For those who dared our deep
  A hundred years ago.

M. A. Sinclair.

The Chatelaine

I have built one, so have you;
Paved with marble, domed with blue,
Battlement and ladies' bower,
Donjon keep and watchman's tower.

I have climbed, as you have done,
To the tower at set of sun --
Crying from its parlous height,
"Watchman, tell us of the night."

I have stolen at midnight bell,
Like you, to the secret cell,
Shuddering at its charnel breath --
Left lockfast the spectre, Death.

I have used your lure to call
Choice guests to my golden hall:
Rarely welcome, rarely free
To my hospitality.

In a glow of rosy light
Hours, like minutes, take their flight --
As from you they fled away,

When, like you, I bade them stay.

Ah! the pretty flow of wit,
And the good hearts under it;
While the wheels of life go round
With a most melodious sound.

Not a vestige anywhere
Of our grim familiar, Care --
Roses! from the trees of yore
Blooming by the rivers four.

Not a jar, and not a fret;
Ecstasy and longing met.
But why should I thus define --
Is not your chateau like mine?

Scarcely were it strange to meet
In that magic realm so sweet,
So! I'll take this dreamland train
Bound for my chateau in Spain.

Sydney Jephcott.

Chaucer

O gracious morning eglantine,
Making the far old English ways divine!
Though from thy stock our mateless rose was bred,
Staining the world's skies with its red,
Our garden gives no scent so fresh as thine,
Sweet, thorny-seeming eglantine.

White Paper

Smooth white paper 'neath the pen;
 Richest field that iron ploughs,
Germinating thoughts of men,
 Though no heaven its rain allows;

Till they ripen, thousand fold,
 And our spirits reap the corn,
In a day-long dream of gold;
 Food for all the souls unborn.

Like the murmur of the earth,
 When we listen stooping low;
Like the sap that sings in mirth,
 Hastening up the trees that grow;

Evermore a tiny song
 Sings the pen unto it, while
Thought's elixir flows along,
 Diviner than the holy Nile.

Greater than the sphering sea,
 For it holds the sea and land;
Seed of all ideas to be
 Down its current borne like sand.

How our fathers in the dark
 Pored on it the plans obscure,
By star-light or stake-fires stark
 Tracing there the path secure.

The poor paper drawn askance
 With the spell of Truth half-known,
Holds back Hell of ignorance,
 Roaring round us, thronged, alone.

O white list of champions,
 Spirit born, and schooled for fight,
Mailed in armour of the sun's
 Who shall win our utmost right!

Think of paper lightly sold,
 Which few pence had made too dear
On its blank to have enscrolled

Beatrice, Lucifer, or Lear!

Think of paper Milton took,
 Written, in his hands to feel,
Musing of what things a look
 Down its pages would reveal.

O the glorious Heaven wrought
 By Cadmean souls of yore,
From pure element of thought!
 And thy leaves they are its door!

Light they open, and we stand
 Past the sovereignty of Fate,
Glad amongst them, calm and grand,
 The Creators and Create!

Splitting

Morning.

 Out from the hut at break of day,
 And up the hills in the dawning grey;
With the young wind flowing
From the blue east, growing
 Red with the white sun's ray!

 Lone and clear as a deep-bright dream
 Under mid-night's and mid-slumber's stream,
Up rises the mount against the sunrise shower,

Vast as a kingdom, fair as a flower:
O'er it doth the foam of foliage ream

In vivid softness serene,
Pearly-purple and marble green;
Clear in their mingling tinges,
Up away to the crest that fringes
Skies studded with cloud-crags sheen.

   Day.

Like birds frayed from their lurking-shaw,
Like ripples fleet 'neath a furious flaw,
The echoes re-echo, flying
Down from the mauls hot-plying;
Clatter the axes, grides the saw.

Ruddy and white the chips out-spring,
Like money sown by a pageant king;
The free wood yields to the driven wedges,
With its white sap-edges,
And heart in the sunshine glistening.

Broadly the ice-clear azure floods down,
Where the great tree-tops are overthrown;
As on through the endless day we labour;
The sun for our nearest neighbour,
Up o'er the mountains lone.

And so intensely it doth illume,
That it shuts by times to gloom;
In the open spaces thrilling;
From the dead leaves distilling

A hot and harsh perfume.

Evening.

Give over! All the valleys in sight
Fill, fill with the rising tide of night;
While the sunset with gold-dust bridges
The black-ravined ridges,
Whose mighty muscles curve in its light.

In our weary climb, while night dyes deep,
Down the broken and stony steep,
How our jaded bodies are shaken
By each step in half-blindness taken --
One's thoughts lie heaped like brutes asleep.

Open the door of the dismal hut,
Silence and darkness lone were shut
In it, as a tidal pool, until returning
Night drowns the land, -- no ember's burning, --
One is too weary the food to cut.

Body and soul with every blow,
Wasted for ever, and who will know,
Where, past this mountained night of toiling,
Red life in its thousand veins is boiling,
Of chips scattered on the mountain's brow?

Home-woe

The wreckage of some name-forgotten barque,
 Half-buried by the dolorous shore;
 Whereto the living waters never more
 Their urgent billows pour;
But the salt spray can reach and cark --

So lies my spirit, lonely and forlorn,
 On Being's strange and perilous strand.
 And rusted sword and fleshless hand
 Point from the smothering sand;
And anchor chainless and out-worn.

But o'er what Deep, unconquered and uncharted,
 And steering by what vanished star;
 And where my dim-imagined consorts are,
 Or hidden harbour far,
From whence my sails, unblessed, departed,

Can memory, nor still intuition teach.
 And so I watch with alien eyes
 This World's remote and unremembered skies;
 While around me weary rise
The babblings of a foreign speech.

A Ballad of the last King of Thule

There was a King of Thule
  Whom a Witch-wife stole at birth;
In a country known but newly,
  All under the dumb, huge Earth.

That King's in a Forest toiling;
  And he never the green sward delves
But he sees all his green waves boiling
  Over his sands and shelves;

In these sunsets vast and fiery,
  In these dawns divine he sees
Hy-Brasil, Mannan and Eire,
  And the Isle of Appletrees;

He watches, heart-still and breathless,
  The clouds through the deep day trailing,
As the white-winged vessels gathered,
  Into his harbours sailing;

Ranked Ibis and lazy Eagles
  In the great blue flame may rise,
But ne'er Sea-mew or Solan beating
  Up through their grey low skies;

When the storm-led fires are breaking,
  Great waves of the molten night,
Deep in his eyes comes aching

The icy Boreal Light.

. . . . .

O, lost King, and O, people perished,
 Your Thule has grown one grave!
Unvisited as uncherished,
 Save by the wandering wave!

The billows burst in his doorways,
 The spray swoops over his walls! --
O, his banners that throb dishonoured
 O'er arms that hide in his halls --

Deserved is your desolation! --
 Why could you not stir and save
The last-born heir of your nation? --
 Sold into the South, a slave

Till he dies, and is buried duly
 In the hot Australian earth --
The lorn, lost King of Thule,
 Whom a Witch-wife stole at birth.

A Fragment

But, under all, my heart believes the day
Was not diviner over Athens, nor

The West wind sweeter thro' the Cyclades
Than here and now; and from the altar of To-day
The eloquent, quick tongues of flame uprise
As fervid, if not unfaltering as of old,
And life atones with speed and plenitude
For coarser texture. Our poor present will,
Far in the brooding future, make a past
Full of the morning's music still, and starred
With great tears shining on the eyelids' eaves
Of our immortal faces yearning t'wards the sun.

Andrew Barton Paterson (`Banjo').

The Daylight is Dying

The daylight is dying
 Away in the west,
The wild birds are flying
 In silence to rest;
In leafage and frondage
 Where shadows are deep,
They pass to their bondage --
 The kingdom of sleep.
And watched in their sleeping
 By stars in the height,

They rest in your keeping,
 Oh, wonderful night.

When night doth her glories
 Of starshine unfold,
'Tis then that the stories
 Of bushland are told.
Unnumbered I hold them
 In memories bright,
But who could unfold them,
 Or read them aright?

Beyond all denials
 The stars in their glories
The breeze in the myalls
 Are part of these stories.
The waving of grasses,
 The song of the river
That sings as it passes
 For ever and ever,
The hobble-chains' rattle,
 The calling of birds,
The lowing of cattle
 Must blend with the words.
Without these, indeed, you
 Would find it ere long,
As though I should read you
 The words of a song
That lamely would linger
 When lacking the rune,
The voice of the singer,
 The lilt of the tune.

But, as one half-hearing
 An old-time refrain,
With memory clearing,
 Recalls it again,
These tales, roughly wrought of
 The bush and its ways,
May call back a thought of
 The wandering days.
And, blending with each
 In the mem'ries that throng,
There haply shall reach
 You some echo of song.

Clancy of the Overflow

I had written him a letter which I had, for want of better
 Knowledge, sent to where I met him down the Lachlan, years ago,
He was shearing when I knew him, so I sent the letter to him,
 Just "on spec", addressed as follows, "Clancy, of The Overflow".

And an answer came directed in a writing unexpected,
 (And I think the same was written with a thumb-nail dipped in tar)
'Twas his shearing mate who wrote it, and verbatim I will quote it:
 "Clancy's gone to Queensland droving, and we don't know where he are."

         .   .   .   .   .

In my wild erratic fancy visions come to me of Clancy
 Gone a-droving "down the Cooper" where the Western drovers go;
As the stock are slowly stringing, Clancy rides behind them singing,

For the drover's life has pleasures that the townsfolk never know.

And the bush hath friends to meet him, and their kindly voices greet him
 In the murmur of the breezes and the river on its bars,
And he sees the vision splendid of the sunlit plains extended,
 And at night the wondrous glory of the everlasting stars.

. . . . .

I am sitting in my dingy little office, where a stingy
 Ray of sunlight struggles feebly down between the houses tall,
And the foetid air and gritty of the dusty, dirty city,
 Through the open window floating, spreads its foulness over all.

And in place of lowing cattle, I can hear the fiendish rattle
 Of the tramways and the 'buses making hurry down the street,
And the language uninviting of the gutter children fighting,
 Comes fitfully and faintly through the ceaseless tramp of feet.

And the hurrying people daunt me, and their pallid faces haunt me
 As they shoulder one another in their rush and nervous haste,
With their eager eyes and greedy, and their stunted forms and weedy,
 For townsfolk have no time to grow, they have no time to waste.

And I somehow rather fancy that I'd like to change with Clancy,
 Like to take a turn at droving where the seasons come and go,
While he faced the round eternal of the cash-book and the journal --
 But I doubt he'd suit the office, Clancy, of "The Overflow".

Black Swans

As I lie at rest on a patch of clover
In the Western Park when the day is done,
I watch as the wild black swans fly over
With their phalanx turned to the sinking sun;
And I hear the clang of their leader crying
To a lagging mate in the rearward flying,
And they fade away in the darkness dying,
Where the stars are mustering one by one.

Oh! ye wild black swans, 'twere a world of wonder
For a while to join in your westward flight,
With the stars above and the dim earth under,
Through the cooling air of the glorious night.
As we swept along on our pinions winging,
We should catch the chime of a church-bell ringing,
Or the distant note of a torrent singing,
Or the far-off flash of a station light.

From the northern lakes with the reeds and rushes,
Where the hills are clothed with a purple haze,
Where the bell-birds chime and the songs of thrushes
Make music sweet in the jungle maze,
They will hold their course to the westward ever,
Till they reach the banks of the old grey river,
Where the waters wash, and the reed-beds quiver
In the burning heat of the summer days.

Oh! ye strange wild birds, will ye bear a greeting

To the folk that live in that western land?
Then for every sweep of your pinions beating,
Ye shall bear a wish to the sunburnt band,
To the stalwart men who are stoutly fighting
With the heat and drought and the dust-storm smiting,
Yet whose life somehow has a strange inviting,
When once to the work they have put their hand.

Facing it yet! Oh, my friend stout-hearted,
What does it matter for rain or shine,
For the hopes deferred and the gain departed?
Nothing could conquer that heart of thine.
And thy health and strength are beyond confessing
As the only joys that are worth possessing.
May the days to come be as rich in blessing
As the days we spent in the auld lang syne.

I would fain go back to the old grey river,
To the old bush days when our hearts were light,
But, alas! those days they have fled for ever,
They are like the swans that have swept from sight.
And I know full well that the strangers' faces
Would meet us now in our dearest places;
For our day is dead and has left no traces
But the thoughts that live in my mind to-night.

There are folk long dead, and our hearts would sicken --
We would grieve for them with a bitter pain,
If the past could live and the dead could quicken,
We then might turn to that life again.
But on lonely nights we would hear them calling,
We should hear their steps on the pathways falling,
We should loathe the life with a hate appalling

In our lonely rides by the ridge and plain.

. . . . .

In the silent park is a scent of clover,
And the distant roar of the town is dead,
And I hear once more as the swans fly over
Their far-off clamour from overhead.
They are flying west, by their instinct guided,
And for man likewise is his fate decided,
And griefs apportioned and joys divided
By a mighty power with a purpose dread.

The Travelling Post Office

The roving breezes come and go, the reed beds sweep and sway,
The sleepy river murmurs low, and loiters on its way,
It is the land of lots o' time along the Castlereagh.

. . . . .

The old man's son had left the farm, he found it dull and slow,
He drifted to the great North-west where all the rovers go.
"He's gone so long," the old man said, "he's dropped right out of mind,
But if you'd write a line to him I'd take it very kind;
He's shearing here and fencing there, a kind of waif and stray,
He's droving now with Conroy's sheep along the Castlereagh.
The sheep are travelling for the grass, and travelling very slow;
They may be at Mundooran now, or past the Overflow,
Or tramping down the black soil flats across by Waddiwong,

But all those little country towns would send the letter wrong,
The mailman, if he's extra tired, would pass them in his sleep,
It's safest to address the note to `Care of Conroy's sheep',
For five and twenty thousand head can scarcely go astray,
You write to `Care of Conroy's sheep along the Castlereagh'."

. . . . .

By rock and ridge and riverside the western mail has gone,
Across the great Blue Mountain Range to take that letter on.
A moment on the topmost grade while open fire doors glare,
She pauses like a living thing to breathe the mountain air,
Then launches down the other side across the plains away
To bear that note to "Conroy's sheep along the Castlereagh".

And now by coach and mailman's bag it goes from town to town,
And Conroy's Gap and Conroy's Creek have marked it "further down".
Beneath a sky of deepest blue where never cloud abides,
A speck upon the waste of plain the lonely mailman rides.
Where fierce hot winds have set the pine and myall boughs asweep
He hails the shearers passing by for news of Conroy's sheep.
By big lagoons where wildfowl play and crested pigeons flock,
By camp fires where the drovers ride around their restless stock,
And past the teamster toiling down to fetch the wool away
My letter chases Conroy's sheep along the Castlereagh.

The Old Australian Ways

The London lights are far abeam
 Behind a bank of cloud,

Along the shore the gaslights gleam,
 The gale is piping loud;
And down the Channel, groping blind,
 We drive her through the haze
Towards the land we left behind --
The good old land of "never mind",
 And old Australian ways.

The narrow ways of English folk
 Are not for such as we;
They bear the long-accustomed yoke
 Of staid conservancy:
But all our roads are new and strange,
 And through our blood there runs
The vagabonding love of change
That drove us westward of the range
 And westward of the suns.

The city folk go to and fro
 Behind a prison's bars,
They never feel the breezes blow
 And never see the stars;
They never hear in blossomed trees
 The music low and sweet
Of wild birds making melodies,
Nor catch the little laughing breeze
 That whispers in the wheat.

Our fathers came of roving stock
 That could not fixed abide:
And we have followed field and flock
 Since e'er we learnt to ride;
By miner's camp and shearing shed,

In land of heat and drought,
We followed where our fortunes led,
With fortune always on ahead
 And always further out.

The wind is in the barley-grass,
 The wattles are in bloom;
The breezes greet us as they pass
 With honey-sweet perfume;
The parrakeets go screaming by
 With flash of golden wing,
And from the swamp the wild-ducks cry
Their long-drawn note of revelry,
 Rejoicing at the Spring.

So throw the weary pen aside
 And let the papers rest,
For we must saddle up and ride
 Towards the blue hill's breast;
And we must travel far and fast
 Across their rugged maze,
To find the Spring of Youth at last,
And call back from the buried past
 The old Australian ways.

When Clancy took the drover's track
 In years of long ago,
He drifted to the outer back
 Beyond the Overflow;
By rolling plain and rocky shelf,
 With stockwhip in his hand,
He reached at last, oh lucky elf!
The Town of Come-and-help-yourself

In Rough-and-ready Land.

And if it be that you would know
 The tracks he used to ride,
Then you must saddle up and go
 Beyond the Queensland side --
Beyond the reach of rule or law,
 To ride the long day through,
In Nature's homestead -- filled with awe:
 You then might see what Clancy saw
 And know what Clancy knew.

By the Grey Gulf-Water

Far to the Northward there lies a land,
 A wonderful land that the winds blow over,
And none may fathom nor understand
 The charm it holds for the restless rover;
A great grey chaos -- a land half made,
 Where endless space is and no life stirreth;
And the soul of a man will recoil afraid
 From the sphinx-like visage that Nature weareth.
But old Dame Nature, though scornful, craves
 Her dole of death and her share of slaughter;
Many indeed are the nameless graves
 Where her victims sleep by the Grey Gulf-water.

Slowly and slowly those grey streams glide,
 Drifting along with a languid motion,
Lapping the reed-beds on either side,

Wending their way to the Northern Ocean.
Grey are the plains where the emus pass
  Silent and slow, with their staid demeanour;
Over the dead men's graves the grass
  Maybe is waving a trifle greener.
Down in the world where men toil and spin
  Dame Nature smiles as man's hand has taught her;
Only the dead men her smiles can win
  In the great lone land by the Grey Gulf-water.

For the strength of man is an insect's strength
  In the face of that mighty plain and river,
And the life of a man is a moment's length
  To the life of the stream that will run for ever.
And so it cometh they take no part
  In small-world worries; each hardy rover
Rideth abroad and is light of heart,
  With the plains around and the blue sky over.
And up in the heavens the brown lark sings
  The songs that the strange wild land has taught her;
Full of thanksgiving her sweet song rings --
  And I wish I were back by the Grey Gulf-water.

Jessie Mackay.

The Grey Company

O the grey, grey company
 Of the pallid dawn!
O the ghostly faces,
 Ashen-like and drawn!
The Lord's lone sentinels
 Dotted down the years,
The little grey company
 Before the pioneers.

Dreaming of Utopias
 Ere the time was ripe,
They awoke to scorning,
 The jeering and the strife.
Dreaming of millenniums
 In a world of wars,
They awoke to shudder
 At a flaming Mars.

Never was a Luther
 But a Huss was first --
A fountain unregarded
 In the primal thirst.

Never was a Newton
 Crowned and honoured well,
But first, alone, Galileo
 Wasted in a cell.

In each other's faces
 Looked the pioneers;
Drank the wine of courage
 All their battle years.
For their weary sowing
 Through the world wide,
Green they saw the harvest
 Ere the day they died.

But the grey, grey company
 Stood every man alone
In the chilly dawnlight,
 Scarcely had they known
Ere the day they perished,
 That their beacon-star
Was not glint of marsh-light
 In the shadows far.

The brave white witnesses
 To the truth within
Took the dart of folly,
 Took the jeer of sin;
Crying "Follow, follow,
 Back to Eden gate!"
They trod the Polar desert,
 Met a desert fate.

Be laurel to the victor,

And roses to the fair,
And asphodel Elysian
   Let the hero wear;
But lay the maiden lilies
   Upon their narrow biers --
The lone grey company
   Before the pioneers.

A Folk Song

I came to your town, my love,
   And you were away, away!
I said "She is with the Queen's maidens:
   They tarry long at their play.
They are stringing her words like pearls
To throw to the dukes and earls."
      But O, the pity!
I had but a morn of windy red
To come to the town where you were bred,
   And you were away, away!

I came to your town, my love,
   And you were away, away!
I said, "She is with the mountain elves
   And misty and fair as they.
They are spinning a diamond net
To cover her curls of jet."
      But O, the pity!
I had but a noon of searing heat
To come to your town, my love, my sweet,

  And you were away, away!

I came to your town, my love,
  And you were away, away!
I said, "She is with the pale white saints,
  And they tarry long to pray.
They give her a white lily-crown,
And I fear she will never come down."
    But O, the pity!
I had but an even grey and wan
To come to your town and plead as man,
  And you were away, away!

Dunedin in the Gloaming

Like a black, enamoured King whispered low the thunder
To the lights of Roslyn, terraced far asunder:
Hovered low the sister cloud in wild, warm wonder.

"O my love, Dunedin town, the only, the abiding!
Who can look undazzled up where the Norn is riding, --
Watch the sword of destiny from the scabbard gliding!

"Dark and rich and ringing true -- word and look for ever;
Taking to her woman heart all forlorn endeavour;
Heaven's sea about her feet, not the bounded river!"

"Sister of the mountain mist, and never to be holden
With the weary sophistries that dimmer eyes embolden, --
O the dark Dunedin town, shot with green and golden!"

Then a silver pioneer netted in the rift,
Leaning over Maori Hill, dreaming in the lift,
Dropped her starry memories through the passioned drift: --

"Once -- I do remember them, the glory and the garden,
Ere the elder stars had learnt God's mystery of pardon,
Ere the youngest, I myself, had seen the flaming warden --

"Once even after even I stole ever shy and early
To mirror me within a glade of Eden cool and pearly,
Where shy and cold and holy ran a torrent sought but rarely.

"And fondly could I swear that this my glade had risen newly, --
Burst the burning desert tomb wherein she lieth truly,
To keep an Easter with the birds and me who loved her duly."

Wailing, laughing, loving, hoar, spake the lordly ocean:
"You are sheen and steadfastness: I am sheen and motion,
Gulfing argosies for whim, navies for a notion.

"Sleep you well, Dunedin Town, though loud the lulling lyre is;
Lady of the stars terrene, where quick the human fire is,
Lady of the Maori pines, the turrets, and the eyries!"

The Burial of Sir John Mackenzie

(1901)

They played him home to the House of Stones
 All the way, all the way,
To his grave in the sound of the winter sea:
 The sky was dour, the sky was gray.
They played him home with the chieftain's dirge,
Till the wail was wed to the rolling surge,
They played him home with a sorrowful will
To his grave at the foot of the Holy Hill
 And the pipes went mourning all the way.

Strong hands that had struck for right
 All the day, all the day,
Folded now in the dark of earth,
 Veiled dawn of the upper way!
Strong hands that struck with his
From days that were to the day that is
Carry him now from the house of woe
To ride the way the Chief must go:
 And his peers went mourning all the way.

Son and brother at his right hand
 All the way, all the way!
And O for them and O for her
 Who stayed within, the dowie day!
Son and brother and near of kin
Go out with the chief who never comes in!

And of all who loved him far and near
'Twas the nearest most who held him dear --
And his kin went mourning all the way!

The clan went on with the pipes before
　All the way, all the way;
A wider clan than ever he knew
　Followed him home that dowie day.
And who were they of the wider clan?
The landless man and the no man's man,
The man that lacked and the man unlearned,
The man that lived but as he earned --
　And the clan went mourning all the way.

The heart of New Zealand went beside
　All the way, all the way,
To the resting-place of her Highland Chief;
　Much she thought she could not say;
He found her a land of many domains,
Maiden forest and fallow plains --
He left her a land of many homes,
The pearl of the world where the sea wind roams,
　And New Zealand went mourning all the way.

Henry Lawson.

Andy's gone with Cattle

Our Andy's gone to battle now
 'Gainst Drought, the red marauder;
Our Andy's gone with cattle now
 Across the Queensland border.

He's left us in dejection now;
 Our hearts with him are roving.
It's dull on this selection now,
 Since Andy went a-droving.

Who now shall wear the cheerful face
 In times when things are slackest?
And who shall whistle round the place
 When Fortune frowns her blackest?

Oh, who shall cheek the squatter now
 When he comes round us snarling?
His tongue is growing hotter now
 Since Andy cross'd the Darling.

The gates are out of order now,
 In storms the "riders" rattle;

For far across the border now
 Our Andy's gone with cattle.

Oh, may the showers in torrents fall,
 And all the tanks run over;
And may the grass grow green and tall
 In pathways of the drover;

And may good angels send the rain
 On desert stretches sandy;
And when the summer comes again
 God grant 'twill bring us Andy.

Out Back

The old year went, and the new returned, in the withering weeks of drought,
The cheque was spent that the shearer earned, and the sheds were all cut out;
The publican's words were short and few,
 and the publican's looks were black --
And the time had come, as the shearer knew, to carry his swag Out Back.

˜For time means tucker, and tramp you must,
 where the scrubs and plains are wide,
With seldom a track that a man can trust, or a mountain peak to guide;
All day long in the dust and heat -- when summer is on the track --
With stinted stomachs and blistered feet, they carry their swags Out Back.˜

He tramped away from the shanty there, when the days were long and hot,
With never a soul to know or care if he died on the track or not.
The poor of the city have friends in woe, no matter how much they lack,

But only God and the swagmen know how a poor man fares Out Back.

He begged his way on the parched Paroo and the Warrego tracks once more,
And lived like a dog, as the swagmen do, till the Western stations shore;
But men were many, and sheds were full, for work in the town was slack --
The traveller never got hands in wool, though he tramped for a year Out Back.

In stifling noons when his back was wrung
  by its load, and the air seemed dead,
And the water warmed in the bag that hung to his aching arm like lead,
Or in times of flood, when plains were seas,
  and the scrubs were cold and black,
He ploughed in mud to his trembling knees, and paid for his sins Out Back.

He blamed himself in the year "Too Late" -- in the heaviest hours of life --
'Twas little he dreamed that a shearing-mate had care of his home and wife;
There are times when wrongs from your kindred come,
  and treacherous tongues attack --
When a man is better away from home, and dead to the world, Out Back.

And dirty and careless and old he wore, as his lamp of hope grew dim;
He tramped for years till the swag he bore seemed part of himself to him.
As a bullock drags in the sandy ruts, he followed the dreary track,
With never a thought but to reach the huts when the sun went down Out Back.

It chanced one day, when the north wind blew
  in his face like a furnace-breath,
He left the track for a tank he knew -- 'twas a short-cut to his death;
For the bed of the tank was hard and dry, and crossed with many a crack,
And, oh! it's a terrible thing to die of thirst in the scrub Out Back.

A drover came, but the fringe of law was eastward many a mile;

He never reported the thing he saw, for it was not worth his while.
The tanks are full and the grass is high in the mulga off the track,
Where the bleaching bones of a white man lie by his mouldering swag Out Back.

~For time means tucker, and tramp they must,
  where the plains and scrubs are wide,
With seldom a track that a man can trust, or a mountain peak to guide;
All day long in the flies and heat the men of the outside track
With stinted stomachs and blistered feet must carry their swags Out Back.~

The Star of Australasia

We boast no more of our bloodless flag, that rose from a nation's slime;
Better a shred of a deep-dyed rag from the storms of the olden time.
From grander clouds in our "peaceful skies" than ever were there before
I tell you the Star of the South shall rise -- in the lurid clouds of war.
It ever must be while blood is warm and the sons of men increase;
For ever the nations rose in storm, to rot in a deadly peace.
There comes a point that we will not yield, no matter if right or wrong,
And man will fight on the battle-field while passion and pride are strong --
So long as he will not kiss the rod, and his stubborn spirit sours,
And the scorn of Nature and curse of God are heavy on peace like ours.

. . . . .

There are boys out there by the western creeks, who hurry away from school
To climb the sides of the breezy peaks or dive in the shaded pool,
Who'll stick to their guns when the mountains quake
  to the tread of a mighty war,

And fight for Right or a Grand Mistake as men never fought before;
When the peaks are scarred and the sea-walls crack
　till the furthest hills vibrate,
And the world for a while goes rolling back in a storm of love and hate.

　　. . . . .

There are boys to-day in the city slum and the home of wealth and pride
Who'll have one home when the storm is come, and fight for it side by side,
Who'll hold the cliffs 'gainst the armoured hells that batter a coastal town,
Or grimly die in a hail of shells when the walls come crashing down.
And many a pink-white baby girl, the queen of her home to-day,
Shall see the wings of the tempest whirl the mist of our dawn away --
Shall live to shudder and stop her ears to the thud of the distant gun,
And know the sorrow that has no tears when a battle is lost and won, --
As a mother or wife in the years to come, will kneel, wild-eyed and white,
And pray to God in her darkened home for the "men in the fort to-night."

　　. . . . .

All creeds and trades will have soldiers there -- give every class its due --
And there'll be many a clerk to spare for the pride of the jackeroo.
They'll fight for honour and fight for love, and a few will fight for gold,
For the devil below and for God above, as our fathers fought of old;
And some half-blind with exultant tears, and some stiff-lipped, stern-eyed,
For the pride of a thousand after-years and the old eternal pride;
The soul of the world they will feel and see
　in the chase and the grim retreat --
They'll know the glory of victory -- and the grandeur of defeat.

The South will wake to a mighty change ere a hundred years are done
With arsenals west of the mountain range and every spur its gun.
And many a rickety "son of a gun", on the tides of the future tossed,

Will tell how battles were really won that History says were lost,
Will trace the field with his pipe, and shirk
  the facts that are hard to explain,
As grey old mates of the diggings work the old ground over again --
How "this was our centre, and this a redoubt,
  and that was a scrub in the rear,
And this was the point where the guards held out,
  and the enemy's lines were here."

    . . . . .

And fools, when the fiends of war are out and the city skies aflame,
Will have something better to talk about than an absent woman's shame,
Will have something nobler to do by far than jest at a friend's expense,
Or blacken a name in a public bar or over a backyard fence.
And this you learn from the libelled past,
  though its methods were somewhat rude --
A nation's born where the shells fall fast, or its lease of life renewed.
We in part atone for the ghoulish strife,
  and the crimes of the peace we boast,
And the better part of a people's life in the storm comes uppermost.

The self-same spirit that drives the man to the depths of drink and crime
Will do the deeds in the heroes' van that live till the end of time.
The living death in the lonely bush, the greed of the selfish town,
And even the creed of the outlawed push is chivalry -- upside down.
'Twill be while ever our blood is hot, while ever the world goes wrong,
The nations rise in a war, to rot in a peace that lasts too long.
And southern nation and southern state, aroused from their dream of ease,
Must sign in the Book of Eternal Fate their stormy histories.

Middleton's Rouseabout

Tall and freckled and sandy,
 Face of a country lout;
This was the picture of Andy,
 Middleton's Rouseabout.

Type of a coming nation,
 In the land of cattle and sheep,
Worked on Middleton's station,
 "Pound a week and his keep."

On Middleton's wide dominions
 Plied the stockwhip and shears;
Hadn't any opinions,
 Hadn't any "idears".

Swiftly the years went over,
 Liquor and drought prevailed;
Middleton went as a drover,
 After his station had failed.

Type of a careless nation,
 Men who are soon played out,
Middleton was: -- and his station
 Was bought by the Rouseabout.

Flourishing beard and sandy,
 Tall and robust and stout;
This is the picture of Andy,
 Middleton's Rouseabout.

Now on his own dominions
  Works with his overseers;
Hasn't any opinions,
  Hasn't any "idears".

The Vagabond

White handkerchiefs wave from the short black pier
 As we glide to the grand old sea --
But the song of my heart is for none to hear
 If one of them waves for me.
A roving, roaming life is mine,
 Ever by field or flood --
For not far back in my father's line
 Was a dash of the Gipsy blood.

Flax and tussock and fern,
 Gum and mulga and sand,
Reef and palm -- but my fancies turn
 Ever away from land;
Strange wild cities in ancient state,
 Range and river and tree,
Snow and ice. But my star of fate
 Is ever across the sea.

A god-like ride on a thundering sea,
 When all but the stars are blind --
A desperate race from Eternity
 With a gale-and-a-half behind.
A jovial spree in the cabin at night,

A song on the rolling deck,
A lark ashore with the ships in sight,
 Till -- a wreck goes down with a wreck.

A smoke and a yarn on the deck by day,
 When life is a waking dream,
And care and trouble so far away
 That out of your life they seem.
A roving spirit in sympathy,
 Who has travelled the whole world o'er --
My heart forgets, in a week at sea,
 The trouble of years on shore.

A rolling stone! -- 'tis a saw for slaves --
 Philosophy false as old --
Wear out or break 'neath the feet of knaves,
 Or rot in your bed of mould!
But I'D rather trust to the darkest skies
 And the wildest seas that roar,
Or die, where the stars of Nations rise,
 In the stormy clouds of war.

Cleave to your country, home, and friends,
 Die in a sordid strife --
You can count your friends on your finger ends
 In the critical hours of life.
Sacrifice all for the family's sake,
 Bow to their selfish rule!
Slave till your big soft heart they break --
 The heart of the family fool.

Domestic quarrels, and family spite,
 And your Native Land may be

Controlled by custom, but, come what might,
　The rest of the world for me.
I'd sail with money, or sail without! --
　If your love be forced from home,
And you dare enough, and your heart be stout,
　The world is your own to roam.

I've never a love that can sting my pride,
　Nor a friend to prove untrue;
For I leave my love ere the turning tide,
　And my friends are all too new.
The curse of the Powers on a peace like ours,
　With its greed and its treachery --
A stranger's hand, and a stranger land,
　And the rest of the world for me!

But why be bitter? The world is cold
　To one with a frozen heart;
New friends are often so like the old,
　They seem of the past a part --
As a better part of the past appears,
　When enemies, parted long,
Are come together in kinder years,
　With their better nature strong.

I had a friend, ere my first ship sailed,
　A friend that I never deserved --
For the selfish strain in my blood prevailed
　As soon as my turn was served.
And the memory haunts my heart with shame --
　Or, rather, the pride that's there;
In different guises, but soul the same,
　I meet him everywhere.

I had a chum. When the times were tight
 We starved in Australian scrubs;
We froze together in parks at night,
 And laughed together in pubs.
And I often hear a laugh like his
 From a sense of humour keen,
And catch a glimpse in a passing phiz
 Of his broad, good-humoured grin.

And I had a love -- 'twas a love to prize --
 But I never went back again . . .
I have seen the light of her kind brown eyes
 In many a face since then.

    .   .   .   .   .

The sailors say 'twill be rough to-night,
 As they fasten the hatches down,
The south is black, and the bar is white,
 And the drifting smoke is brown.
The gold has gone from the western haze,
 The sea-birds circle and swarm --
But we shall have plenty of sunny days,
 And little enough of storm.

The hill is hiding the short black pier,
 As the last white signal's seen;
The points run in, and the houses veer,
 And the great bluff stands between.
So darkness swallows each far white speck
 On many a wharf and quay.
The night comes down on a restless deck, --

Grim cliffs -- and -- The Open Sea!

The Sliprails and the Spur

The colours of the setting sun
  Withdrew across the Western land --
He raised the sliprails, one by one,
  And shot them home with trembling hand;
Her brown hands clung -- her face grew pale --
  Ah! quivering chin and eyes that brim! --
One quick, fierce kiss across the rail,
  And, "Good-bye, Mary!" "Good-bye, Jim!"
    ~Oh, he rides hard to race the pain
      Who rides from love, who rides from home;
     But he rides slowly home again,
      Whose heart has learnt to love and roam.~

A hand upon the horse's mane,
  And one foot in the stirrup set,
And, stooping back to kiss again,
  With "Good-bye, Mary! don't you fret!
When I come back" -- he laughed for her --
  "We do not know how soon 'twill be;
I'll whistle as I round the spur --
  You let the sliprails down for me."

She gasped for sudden loss of hope,
  As, with a backward wave to her,
He cantered down the grassy slope
  And swiftly round the dark'ning spur.

Black-pencilled panels standing high,
 And darkness fading into stars,
And blurring fast against the sky,
 A faint white form beside the bars.

And often at the set of sun,
 In winter bleak and summer brown,
She'd steal across the little run,
 And shyly let the sliprails down.
And listen there when darkness shut
 The nearer spur in silence deep;
And when they called her from the hut
 Steal home and cry herself to sleep.

. . . . .

~And he rides hard to dull the pain
 Who rides from one that loves him best;
And he rides slowly back again,
 Whose restless heart must rove for rest.~

Arthur Albert Dawson Bayldon.

Sunset

The weary wind is slumbering on the wing:
Leaping from out meek twilight's purpling blue
Burns the proud star of eve as though it knew
It was the big king jewel quivering
On the black turban of advancing night.
In the dim west the soldiers of the sun
Strike all their royal colours one by one,
Reluctantly surrender every height.

The Sea

Ere Greece soared, showering sovranties of light,
Ere Rome shook earth with her tremendous tread,
Ere yon blue-feasting sun-god burst blood-red,
Beneath thee slept thy prodigy, O Night!
Aeons have ta'en like dreams their strange, slow flight,
And vastest, tiniest, creatures paved her bed,
E'en cities sapped by the usurping spread
Of her imperious waves have sunk from sight

Since she first chanted her colossal psalms
That swell and sink beneath the listening stars;
Oft, as with myriad drums beating to arms,
She thunders out the grandeur of her wars;
Then shifts through moaning moods her wizard charms
Of slow flutes and caressing, gay guitars.

To Poesy

These vessels of verse, O Great Goddess, are filled with invisible tears,
With the sobs and sweat of my spirit and her desolate brooding for years;
See, I lay them -- not on thine altar, for they are unpolished and plain,
Not rounded enough by the potter, too much burnt in the furnace of pain;
But here in the dust, in the shadow, with a sudden wild leap of the heart
I kneel to tenderly kiss them, then in silence arise to depart.

I linger awhile at the portal with the light of the crimsoning sun
On my wreathless brow bearing the badges of battles I've fought in not won.
At the sound of the trumpet I've ever been found in thy thin fighting line,
And the weapons I've secretly sharpened have flashed in defence of thy shrine.
I've recked not of failure and losses, nor shrunk from the soilure of strife
For thy magical glamour was on me and art is the moonlight of life.

I move from the threshold, Great Goddess, with steps meditative and slow;
Night steals like a dream to the landscape and slips like a pall
  o'er its glow.
I carry no lamp in my bosom and dwindling in gloom is the track,
No token of man's recognition to prompt me to ever turn back.
I strike eastward to meet the great day-dawn with the soul of my soul
  by my side,

My goal though unknown is assured me, and the planet of Love is my guide.

Jennings Carmichael.

An Old Bush Road

Dear old road, wheel-worn and broken,
 Winding thro' the forest green,
Barred with shadow and with sunshine,
 Misty vistas drawn between.
Grim, scarred bluegums ranged austerely,
 Lifting blackened columns each
To the large, fair fields of azure,
 Stretching ever out of reach.

See the hardy bracken growing
 Round the fallen limbs of trees;
And the sharp reeds from the marshes,
 Washed across the flooded leas;
And the olive rushes, leaning
 All their pointed spears to cast
Slender shadows on the roadway,
 While the faint, slow wind creeps past.

Ancient ruts grown round with grasses,

Soft old hollows filled with rain;
Rough, gnarled roots all twisting queerly,
 Dark with many a weather-stain.
Lichens moist upon the fences,
 Twiners close against the logs;
Yellow fungus in the thickets,
 Vivid mosses in the bogs.

Dear old road, wheel-worn and broken,
 What delights in thee I find!
Subtle charm and tender fancy,
 Like a fragrance in the mind.
Thy old ways have set me dreaming,
 And out-lived illusions rise,
And the soft leaves of the landscape
 Open on my thoughtful eyes.

See the clump of wattles, standing
 Dead and sapless on the rise;
When their boughs were full of beauty,
 Even to uncaring eyes,
I was ever first to rifle
 The soft branches of their store.
O the golden wealth of blossom
 I shall gather there no more!

Now we reach the dun morasses,
 Where the red moss used to grow,
Ruby-bright upon the water,
 Floating on the weeds below.
Once the swan and wild-fowl glided
 By those sedges, green and tall;
Here the booming bitterns nested;

Here we heard the curlews call.

Climb this hill and we have rambled
 To the last turn of the way;
Here is where the bell-birds tinkled
 Fairy chimes for me all day.
These were bells that never wearied,
 Swung by ringers on the wing;
List! the elfin strains are waking,
 Memory sets the bells a-ring!

Dear old road, no wonder, surely,
 That I love thee like a friend!
And I grieve to think how surely
 All thy loveliness will end.
For thy simple charm is passing,
 And the turmoil of the street
Soon will mar thy sylvan silence
 With the tramp of careless feet.

And for this I look more fondly
 On the sunny landscape, seen
From the road, wheel-worn and broken,
 Winding thro' the forest green,
Something still remains of Nature,
 Thoughts of other days to bring: --
For the staunch old trees are standing,
 And I hear the wild birds sing!

A Woman's Mood

I think to-night I could bear it all,
 Even the arrow that cleft the core, --
Could I wait again for your swift footfall,
 And your sunny face coming in at the door.
With the old frank look and the gay young smile,
 And the ring of the words you used to say;
I could almost deem the pain worth while,
 To greet you again in the olden way!

But you stand without in the dark and cold,
 And I may not open the long closed door,
Nor call thro' the night, with the love of old, --
 "Come into the warmth, as in nights of yore!"
I kneel alone in the red fire-glow,
 And hear the wings of the wind sweep by;
You are out afar in the night, I know,
 And the sough of the wind is like a cry.

You are out afar -- and I wait within,
 A grave-eyed woman whose pulse is slow;
The flames round the red coals softly spin,
 And the lonely room's in a rosy glow.
The firelight falls on your vacant chair,
 And the soft brown rug where you used to stand;
Dear, never again shall I see you there,
 Nor lift my head for your seeking hand.

Yet sometimes still, and in spite of all,

I wistful look at the fastened door,
And wait again for the swift footfall,
  And the gay young voice as in hours of yore.
It still seems strange to be here alone,
  With the rising sob of the wind without;
The sound takes a deep, insisting tone,
  Where the trees are swinging their arms about.

Its moaning reaches the sheltered room,
  And thrills my heart with a sense of pain;
I walk to the window, and pierce the gloom,
  With a yearning look that is all in vain.
You are out in a night of depths that hold
  No promise of dawning for you and me,
And only a ghost from the life of old
  Has come from the world of memory!

You are out evermore! God wills it so!
  But ah! my spirit is yearning yet!
As I kneel alone by the red fire-glow,
  My eyes grow dim with the old regret.
O when shall the aching throb grow still,
  The warm love-life turn cold at the core!
Must I be watching, against my will,
  For your banished face in the opening door?

It may be, dear, when the sequel's told
  Of the story, read to its bitter close;
When the inner meanings of life unfold,
  And the under-side of our being shows --
It may be then, in that truer light,
  When all our knowledge has larger grown,
I may understand why you stray to-night,

And I am left, with the past, alone.

Agnes L. Storrie.

Twenty Gallons of Sleep

Measure me out from the fathomless tun
 That somewhere or other you keep
In your vasty cellars, O wealthy one,
 Twenty gallons of sleep.

Twenty gallons of balmy sleep,
 Dreamless, and deep, and mild,
Of the excellent brand you used to keep
 When I was a little child.

I've tasted of all your vaunted stock,
 Your clarets and ports of Spain,
The liquid gold of your famous hock,
 And your matchless dry champagne.

Of your rich muscats and your sherries fine,
 I've drunk both well and deep,
Then, measure me out, O merchant mine,
 Twenty gallons of sleep.

Twenty gallons of slumber soft
 Of the innocent, baby kind,
When the angels flutter their wings aloft
 And the pillow with down is lined;

I have drawn the corks, and drained the lees
 Of every vintage pressed,
If I've felt the sting of my honey bees
 I've taken it with the rest.

I have lived my life, and I'll not repine,
 As I sowed I was bound to reap;
Then, measure me out, O merchant mine,
 Twenty gallons of sleep.

A Confession

You did not know, -- how could you, dear, --
How much you stood for? Life in you
Retained its touch of Eden dew,
And ever through the droughtiest year
My soul could bring her flagon here
And fill it to the brim with clear
   Deep draughts of purity:
And time could never quench the flame
Of youth that lit me through your eyes,
And cozened winter from my skies
Through all the years that went and came.
You did not know I used your name

To conjure by, and still the same
  I found its potency.
You did not know that, as a phial
May garner close through dust and gloom
The essence of a rich perfume,
Romance was garnered in your smile
And touched my thoughts with beauty, while
The poor world, wise with bitter guile,
  Outlived its chivalry.
You did not know -- our lives were laid
So far apart -- that thus I drew
The sunshine of my days from you,
That by your joy my own was weighed
That thus my debts your sweetness paid,
And of my heart's deep silence made
  A lovely melody.

Martha M. Simpson.

To an Old Grammar

Oh, mighty conjuror, you raise
  The ghost of my lost youth --
The happy, golden-tinted days
When earth her treasure-trove displays,

And everything is truth.

Your compeers may be sage and dry,
 But in your page appears
A very fairyland, where I
Played 'neath a changeful Irish sky --
 A sky of smiles and tears.

Dear native land! this little book
 Brings back the varied charm
Of emerald hill and flashing brook,
Deep mountain glen and woodland nook,
 And homely sheltered farm.

I see the hayrick where I sat
 In golden autumn days,
And conned thy page, and wondered what
Could be the use, excepting that
 It gained the master's praise.

I conjugate thy verbs again
 Beside the winter's fire,
And, as the solemn clock strikes ten,
I lay thee on the shelf, and then
 To dreams of thee retire.

Thy Saxon roots reveal to me
 A silent, empty school,
And one poor prisoner who could see,
As if to increase her misery,
 Her mates released from rule,

Rushing to catch the rounder ball,

Or circling in the ring.
Those merry groups! I see them all,
And even now I can recall
  The songs they used to sing.

Thy syntax conjures forth a morn
  Of spring, when blossoms rare
Conspired the solemn earth to adorn,
And spread themselves on bank and thorn,
  And perfumed all the air.

The dewdrops lent their aid and threw
  Their gems with lavish hand
On every flower of brilliant hue,
On every blade of grass that grew
  In that enchanted land.

The lark her warbling music lent,
  To give an added charm,
And sleek-haired kine, in deep content,
Forth from their milking slowly went
  Towards the homestead farm.

And here thy page on logic shows
  A troop of merry girls,
A meadow smooth where clover grows,
And lanes where scented hawthorn blows,
  And woodbine twines and curls.

And, turning o'er thy leaves, I find
  Of many a friend the trace;
Forgotten scenes rush to my mind,
And some whom memory left behind

Now stare me in the face.

. . . . .

Ah, happy days! when hope was high,
 And faith was calm and deep!
When all was real and God was nigh,
And heaven was "just beyond the sky",
 And angels watched my sleep.

Your dreams are gone, and here instead
 Fair science reigns alone,
And, when I come to her for bread,
She smiles and bows her stately head
 And offers me -- a stone.

William Gay.

Primroses

They shine upon my table there,
 A constellation mimic sweet,
No stars in Heaven could shine more fair,
 Nor Earth has beauty more complete;
And on my table there they shine,

And speak to me of things Divine.

In Heaven at first they grew, and when
 God could no fairer make them, He
Did plant them by the ways of men
 For all the pure in heart to see,
That each might shine upon its stem
And be a light from Him to them.

They speak of things above my verse,
 Of thoughts no earthly language knows,
That loftiest Bard could ne'er rehearse,
 Nor holiest prophet e'er disclose,
Which God Himself no other way
Than by a Primrose could convey.

To M.

(With some Verses)

If in the summer of thy bright regard
 For one brief season these poor Rhymes shall live
I ask no more, nor think my fate too hard
 If other eyes but wintry looks should give;
Nor will I grieve though what I here have writ
 O'erburdened Time should drop among the ways,
And to the unremembering dust commit
 Beyond the praise and blame of other days:
The song doth pass, but I who sing, remain,
 I pluck from Death's own heart a life more deep,

And as the Spring, that dies not, in her train
 Doth scatter blossoms for the winds to reap,
So I, immortal, as I fare along,
Will strew my path with mortal flowers of song.

Vestigia Nulla Retrorsum

O steep and rugged Life, whose harsh ascent
 Slopes blindly upward through the bitter night!
 They say that on thy summit, high in light,
Sweet rest awaits the climber, travel-spent;
But I, alas, with dusty garments rent,
 With fainting heart and failing limbs and sight,
 Can see no glimmer of the shining height,
And vainly list, with body forward bent,
To catch athwart the gloom one wandering note
 Of those glad anthems which (they say) are sung
  When one emerges from the mists below:
But though, O Life, thy summit be remote
 And all thy stony path with darkness hung,
  Yet ever upward through the night I go.

Edward Dyson.

The Old Whim Horse

He's an old grey horse, with his head bowed sadly,
  And with dim old eyes and a queer roll aft,
With the off-fore sprung and the hind screwed badly,
  And he bears all over the brands of graft;
And he lifts his head from the grass to wonder
  Why by night and day the whim is still,
Why the silence is, and the stampers' thunder
  Sounds forth no more from the shattered mill.

In that whim he worked when the night winds bellowed
  On the riven summit of Giant's Hand,
And by day when prodigal Spring had yellowed
  All the wide, long sweep of enchanted land;
And he knew his shift, and the whistle's warning,
  And he knew the calls of the boys below;
Through the years, unbidden, at night or morning,
  He had taken his stand by the old whim bow.

But the whim stands still, and the wheeling swallow
  In the silent shaft hangs her home of clay,
And the lizards flirt and the swift snakes follow
  O'er the grass-grown brace in the summer day;

And the corn springs high in the cracks and corners
 Of the forge, and down where the timber lies;
And the crows are perched like a band of mourners
 On the broken hut on the Hermit's Rise.

All the hands have gone, for the rich reef paid out,
 And the company waits till the calls come in;
But the old grey horse, like the claim, is played out,
 And no market's near for his bones and skin.
So they let him live, and they left him grazing
 By the creek, and oft in the evening dim
I have seen him stand on the rises, gazing
 At the ruined brace and the rotting whim.

The floods rush high in the gully under,
 And the lightnings lash at the shrinking trees,
Or the cattle down from the ranges blunder
 As the fires drive by on the summer breeze.
Still the feeble horse at the right hour wanders
 To the lonely ring, though the whistle's dumb,
And with hanging head by the bow he ponders
 Where the whim boy's gone -- why the shifts don't come.

But there comes a night when he sees lights glowing
 In the roofless huts and the ravaged mill,
When he hears again all the stampers going --
 Though the huts are dark and the stampers still:
When he sees the steam to the black roof clinging
 As its shadows roll on the silver sands,
And he knows the voice of his driver singing,
 And the knocker's clang where the braceman stands.

See the old horse take, like a creature dreaming,

On the ring once more his accustomed place;
But the moonbeams full on the ruins streaming
  Show the scattered timbers and grass-grown brace.
Yet HE hears the sled in the smithy falling,
  And the empty truck as it rattles back,
And the boy who stands by the anvil, calling;
  And he turns and backs, and he "takes up slack".

While the old drum creaks, and the shadows shiver
  As the wind sweeps by, and the hut doors close,
And the bats dip down in the shaft or quiver
  In the ghostly light, round the grey horse goes;
And he feels the strain on his untouched shoulder,
  Hears again the voice that was dear to him,
Sees the form he knew -- and his heart grows bolder
  As he works his shift by the broken whim.

He hears in the sluices the water rushing
  As the buckets drain and the doors fall back;
When the early dawn in the east is blushing,
  He is limping still round the old, old track.
Now he pricks his ears, with a neigh replying
  To a call unspoken, with eyes aglow,
And he sways and sinks in the circle, dying;
  From the ring no more will the grey horse go.

In a gully green, where a dam lies gleaming,
  And the bush creeps back on a worked-out claim,
And the sleepy crows in the sun sit dreaming
  On the timbers grey and a charred hut frame,
Where the legs slant down, and the hare is squatting
  In the high rank grass by the dried-up course,
Nigh a shattered drum and a king-post rotting

Are the bleaching bones of the old grey horse.

Dowell O'Reilly.

The Sea-Maiden

Like summer waves on sands of snow,
Soft ringlets clasp her neck and brow,
And wandering breezes kiss away
A threaded light of glimmering spray,
That drifts and floats and softly flies
In a golden mist about her eyes.
Her laugh is fresh as foam that springs
Through tumbling shells and shining things,
And where the gleaming margin dries
Is heard the music of her sighs.
Her gentle bosom ebbs and swells
With the tide of life that deeply wells
From a throbbing heart that loves to break
In the tempest of love for love's sweet sake.
O, the fragrance of earth, and the song of the sea,
And the light of the heavens, are only three
Of the thousand glories that Love can trace,
In her life, and her soul, and her beautiful face.

. . . . .

This tangled weed of poesy,
Torn from the heart of a stormy sea,
I fling upon the love divine
Of her, who fills this heart of mine.

David MacDonald Ross.

Love's Treasure House

I went to Love's old treasure house last night,
Alone, when all the world was still -- asleep,
And saw the miser Memory, grown gray
With years of jealous counting of his gems,
There seated. Keen was his eye, his hand
Firm as when first his hoarding he began
Of precious things of Love, long years ago.
"And this," he said, "is gold from out her hair,
And this the moonlight that she wandered in,
With here a rose, enamelled by her breath,
That bloomed in glory 'tween her breasts, and here
The brimming sun-cup that she quaffed at noon,
And here the star that cheered her in the night;
In this great chest, see curiously wrought,

Are purest of Love's gems." A ruby key,
Enclasped upon a golden ring, he took,
With care, from out some secret hiding-place,
And delicately touched the lock, whereat
I staggered, blinded by the light of things
More luminous than stars, and questioned thus --
"What are these treasures, miser Memory?"
And slowly bending his gray head, he spoke:
"These are the multitudes of kisses sweet
Love gave so gladly, and I treasure here."

The Sea to the Shell

The sea, my mother, is singing to me,
 She is singing the old refrain,
Of passion, of love, and of mystery,
 And her world-old song of pain;
Of the mirk midnight and the dazzling day,
That trail their robes o'er the wet sea-way.

The sea, my mother, is singing to me
 With the white foam caught in her hair,
With the seaweed swinging its long arms free,
 To grapple the blown sea air:
The sea, my mother, with billowy swell,
Is telling her tale to the wave-washed shell.

The sea, my mother, is singing to me,
 With the starry gleam in her wave,
A dirge of the dead, of the sad, sad sea,

A requiem song of the brave;
Tenderly, sadly, the surges tell
Their tale of death to the wave-washed shell.

The sea, my mother, confides to me,
 As she turns to the soft, round moon,
The secrets that lie where the spirits be,
 That hide from the garish noon:
The sea, my mother, who loves me well,
Is telling their woe to the wave-washed shell.

O mother o' mine, with the foam-flecked hair,
 O mother, I love and know
The heart that is sad and the soul that is bare
 To your daughter of ebb and flow;
And I hold your whispers of Heaven and Hell
In the loving heart of a wave-washed shell.

The Silent Tide

I heard Old Ocean raise her voice and cry,
 In that still hour between the night and day;
 I saw the answering tides, green robed and gray,
Turn to her with a low contented sigh;
Marching with silent feet they passed me by,
 For the white moon had taught them to obey,
 And scarce a wavelet broke in fretful spray,
As they went forth to kiss the stooping sky.

So, to my heart, when the last sunray sleeps,

And the wan night, impatient for the moon,
Throws her gray mantle over land and sea,
There comes a call from out Life's nether deeps,
  And tides, like some old ocean in a swoon,
Flow out, in soundless majesty, to thee.

The Watch on Deck

Becalmed upon the equatorial seas,
 A ship of gold lay on a sea of fire;
 Each sail and rope and spar, as in desire,
Mutely besought the kisses of a breeze;
Low laughter told the mariners at ease;
 Sweet sea-songs hymned the red sun's fun'ral pyre:
 Yet One, with eyes that never seemed to tire,
Watched for the storm, nursed on the thunder's knees.

Thou watcher of the spirit's inner keep,
Scanning Death's lone, illimitable deep,
 Spread outward to the far immortal shore!
While the vault sleeps, from the upheaving deck,
Thou see'st the adamantine reefs that wreck,
 And Life's low shoals, where lusting billows roar.

Autumn

When, with low moanings on the distant shore,
 Like vain regrets, the ocean-tide is rolled:
 When, thro' bare boughs, the tale of death is told
By breezes sighing, "Summer days are o'er";
When all the days we loved -- the days of yore --
 Lie in their vaults, dead Kings who ruled of old --
 Unrobed and sceptreless, uncrowned with gold,
Conquered, and to be crowned, ah! never more.

If o'er the bare fields, cold and whitening
 With the first snow-flakes, I should see thy form,
And meet and kiss thee, that were enough of Spring;
 Enough of sunshine, could I feel the warm
Glad beating of thy heart 'neath Winter's wing,
 Tho' Earth were full of whirlwind and of storm.

Mary Gilmore.

A Little Ghost

The moonlight flutters from the sky
 To meet her at the door,
A little ghost, whose steps have passed
 Across the creaking floor.

And rustling vines that lightly tap
 Against the window-pane,
Throw shadows on the white-washed walls
 To blot them out again.

The moonlight leads her as she goes
 Across a narrow plain,
By all the old, familiar ways
 That know her steps again.

And through the scrub it leads her on
 And brings her to the creek,
But by the broken dam she stops
 And seems as she would speak.

She moves her lips, but not a sound
 Ripples the silent air;
She wrings her little hands, ah, me!

The sadness of despair!

While overhead the black-duck's wing
 Cuts like a flash upon
The startled air, that scarcely shrinks
 Ere he afar is gone.

And curlews wake, and wailing cry
 Cur-lew! cur-lew! cur-lew!
Till all the Bush, with nameless dread
 Is pulsing through and through.

The moonlight leads her back again
 And leaves her at the door,
A little ghost whose steps have passed
 Across the creaking floor.

Good-Night

Good-night! . . . my darling sleeps so sound
She cannot hear me where she lies;
White lilies watch the closed eyes,
Red roses guard the folded hands.

Good-night! O woman who once lay
Upon my breast, so still, so sweet
That all my pulses, throbbing, beat
And flamed -- I cannot touch you now.

Good-night, my own! God knows we loved

So well, that all things else seemed slight --
We part forever in the night,
We two poor souls who loved so well.

Bernard O'Dowd.

Love's Substitute

This love, that dares not warm before its flame
 Our yearning hands, or from its tempting tree
Yield fruit we may consume, or let us claim
 In Hymen's scroll of happy heraldry
 The twining glyphs of perfect you and me --
May kindle social fires whence curls no blame,
 Find gardens where no fruits forbidden be,
And mottoes weave, unsullied by a shame.

For, love, unmothered Childhood wanly waits
 For such as you to cherish it to Youth:
  Raw social soils untilled need Love's own verve
That Peace a-flower may oust their weedy hates:
 And where Distress would faint from wolfish sleuth
  The perfect lovers' symbol is "We serve!"

Our Duty

Yet what were Love if man remains unfree,
  And woman's sunshine sordid merchandise:
If children's Hope is blasted ere they see
  Its shoots of youth from out the branchlets rise:
  If thought is chained, and gagged is Speech, and Lies
Enthroned as Law befoul posterity,
  And haggard Sin's ubiquitous disguise
Insults the face of God where'er men be?

Ay, what were Love, my love, did we not love
  Our stricken brothers so, as to resign
  For Its own sake, the foison of Its dower:
That, so, we two may help them mount above
  These layers of charnel air in which they pine,
  To seek with us the Presence and the Power?

Edwin James Brady.

The Wardens of the Seas

Like star points in the ether to guide a homing soul
Towards God's Eternal Haven; above the wash and roll,
Across and o'er the oceans, on all the coasts they stand
Tall seneschals of commerce, High Wardens of the Strand --
    The white lights slowly turning
    Their kind eyes far and wide,
    The red and green lights burning
    Along the waterside.

When Night with breath of aloes, magnolia, spice, and balm
Creeps down the darkened jungles and mantles reef and palm,
By velvet waters making soft music as they surge
The shore lights of dark Asia will one by one emerge --
    Oh, Ras Marshig by Aden
    Shows dull on hazy nights;
    And Bombay Channel's laid in
    Its "In" and "Outer" lights.

When Night, in rain-wet garments comes sobbing cold and grey
Across the German Ocean and South from Stornoway,
Thro' snarling darkness slowly, some fixed and some a-turn,
The bright shore-lights of Europe like welcome tapers burn, --
    From fierce Fruholmen streaming

O'er Northern ice and snow,
To Cape St. Vincent gleaming, --
These lamps of danger glow.

The dark Etruscan tending his watchfires by the shore,
On sacred altars burning, the world shall know no more;
His temple's column standing against the ancient stars
Is gone; Now bright catoptrics flash out electric bars, --
   Slow swung his stately Argos
   Unto the Tiber's mouth;
   But now the Tuscan cargoes
   Screw-driven, stagger South.

The lantern of Genoa guides home no Eastern fleets
As when the boy Columbus played in its narrow streets:
No more the Keltic `dolmens' their fitful warnings throw
Across the lone Atlantic, so long, so long ago --
   No more the beaked prows dashing
   Shall dare a shoreward foam;
   No more will great oars threshing
   Sweep Dorian galleys home.

No more the Vikings roaring their sagas wild and weird
Proclaim that Rome has fallen; no more a consul feared
Shall quench the Roman pharos lest Northern pirates free
Be pointed to their plunder on coasts of Italy --
   Nor shall unwilling lovers,
   From Lethean pleasures torn,
   Fare nor'ward with those rovers,
   To frozen lands forlorn.

The bale-fires and the watch-fires, the wrecker's foul false lure
No more shall vex the shipmen; and on their course secure

Past Pharos in the starlight the tow'ring hulls of Trade
Race in and out from Suez in iron cavalcade, --
   So rode one sunset olden
   Across the dark'ning sea,
   With banners silk and golden,
   The Barge of Antony!

They loom along the foreshores; they gleam across the Straits;
They guide the feet of Commerce unto the harbor gates.
In nights of storm and thunder, thro' fog and sleet and rain,
Like stars on angels' foreheads, they give man heart again, --
   Oh, hear the high waves smashing
   On Patagonia's shore!
   Oh, hear the black waves threshing
   Their weight on Skerryvore!

He searches night's grim chances upon his bridge alone
And seeks the distant glimmer of hopeful Eddystone:
And thro' a thick fog creeping, with chart and book and lead,
The homeward skipper follows their green and white and red --
   By day his lighthouse wardens
   In sunlit quiet stand,
   But in the night the burdens
   Are theirs of Sea and Land.

They fill that night with Knowledge. A thousand ships go by,
A thousand captains bless them, so bright and proud and high:
The world's dark capes they glamour; or low on sand banks dread,
They, crouching, mark a pathway between the Quick and Dead --
   Like star points in the ether
   They bring the seamen ease,
   These Lords of Wind and Weather
   These Wardens of the Seas!

Will. H. Ogilvie.

Queensland Opal

Opal, little opal, with the red fire glancing,
 Set my blood a-spinning, set my pulse a-stir,
Strike the harp of memory, set my dull heart dancing
 Southward to the Sunny Land and the love of Her!

Opal, shining opal, let them call you luckless jewel,
 Let them curse or let them covet, you are still my heart's desire,
You that robbed the sun and moon and green earth for fuel
 To gather to your milky breast and fill your veins with fire!

Green of fluttering gum-leaves above dim water-courses,
 Red of rolling dust-clouds, blue of summer skies,
Flash of flints afire beneath the hoofs of racing horses,
 Sunlight and moonlight and light of lovers' eyes

Pink clasping hands amid a Southern summer gloaming,
 Green of August grasses, white of dew-sprung pearls,
Grey of winging wild geese into the Sunset homing,
 Twined with all the kisses of a Queen of Queensland girls!

Wind o' the Autumn

I love you, wind o' the Autumn, that came from I know not where,
To lead me out of the toiling world to a ballroom fresh and fair,
Where the poplars tall and golden and the beeches rosy and red
Are setting to woodland partners and dancing the stars to bed!

Oh! say, wild wind o' the Autumn, may I dance this dance with you
Decked out in your gown of moonmist and jewelled with drops of dew?
For I know no waiting lover with arms that so softly twine,
And I know no dancing partner whose step is so made for mine!

Daffodils

Ho! You there, selling daffodils along the windy street,
Poor drooping, dusty daffodils -- but oh! so Summer sweet!
Green stems that stab with loveliness, rich petal-cups to hold
The wine of Spring to lips that cling like bees about their gold!

What price to you for daffodils? I'll give what price you please,
For light and love and memory lie leaf by leaf with these!
And if I bought all Sydney Town I could not hope to buy
The wealth you bring of everything that goes with open sky!

My money for your daffodils: why do you thank me so?
If I have paid a reckless price, take up my gift and go,

And from the golden garden beds where gold the sunbeams shine
Bring in more flowers to light the hours for lover-hearts like mine!

A Queen of Yore

Slowly she hobbles past the town, grown old at heart and gray;
With misty eyes she stumbles down along the well-known way;
She sees her maiden march unrolled by billabong and bend,
And every gum's a comrade old and every oak's a friend;
But gone the smiling faces that welcomed her of yore --
They crowd her tented places and hold her hand no more.
And she, the friend they once could trust to serve their eager wish,
Shall show no more the golden dust that hides in many a dish;
And through the dismal mullock-heaps she threads her mournful way
Where here and there some gray-beard keeps his windlass-watch to-day;
Half-flood no more she looses her reins as once of old
To wash the busy sluices and whisper through the gold.
She sees no wild-eyed steers above stand spear-horned on the brink;
The brumby mobs she used to love come down no more to drink;
Where green the grasses used to twine above them, shoulder-deep,
Through the red dust -- a long, slow line -- crawl in the starving sheep;
She sees no crossing cattle that Western drovers bring,
No swimming steeds that battle to block them when they ring.

She sees no barricaded roofs, no loop-holed station wall,
No foaming steed with flying hoofs to bring the word "Ben Hall!"
She sees no reckless robbers stoop behind their ambush stone,
No coach-and-four, no escort troop; -- but, very lorn and lone,
Watches the sunsets redden along the mountain side
Where round the spurs of Weddin the wraiths of Weddin ride.

Tho' fettered with her earthen bars and chained with bridge and weir
She goes her own way with the stars; she knows the course to steer!
And when her thousand rocky rills foam, angry, to her feet,
Rain-heavy from the Cowra hills she takes her vengeance sweet,
And leaps with roar of thunder, and buries bridge and ford,
That all the world may wonder when the Lachlan bares her sword!

Gray River! let me take your hand for all your memories old --
Your cattle-kings, your outlaw-band, your wealth of virgin gold;
For once you held, and hold it now, the sceptre of a queen,
And still upon your furrowed brow the royal wreaths are green;
Hold wide your arms, the waters! Lay bare your silver breast
To nurse the sons and daughters that spread your empire west!

Drought

My road is fenced with the bleached, white bones
 And strewn with the blind, white sand,
Beside me a suffering, dumb world moans
 On the breast of a lonely land.

On the rim of the world the lightnings play,
 The heat-waves quiver and dance,
And the breath of the wind is a sword to slay
 And the sunbeams each a lance.

I have withered the grass where my hot hoofs tread,
 I have whitened the sapless trees,
I have driven the faint-heart rains ahead

To hide in their soft green seas.

I have bound the plains with an iron band,
  I have stricken the slow streams dumb!
To the charge of my vanguards who shall stand?
  Who stay when my cohorts come?

The dust-storms follow and wrap me round;
  The hot winds ride as a guard;
Before me the fret of the swamps is bound
  And the way of the wild-fowl barred.

I drop the whips on the loose-flanked steers;
  I burn their necks with the bow;
And the green-hide rips and the iron sears
  Where the staggering, lean beasts go.

I lure the swagman out of the road
  To the gleam of a phantom lake;
I have laid him down, I have taken his load,
  And he sleeps till the dead men wake.

My hurrying hoofs in the night go by,
  And the great flocks bleat their fear
And follow the curve of the creeks burnt dry
  And the plains scorched brown and sere.

The worn men start from their sleepless rest
  With faces haggard and drawn;
They cursed the red Sun into the west
  And they curse him out of the dawn.

They have carried their outposts far, far out,

But -- blade of my sword for a sign! --
I am the Master, the dread King Drought,
And the great West Land is mine!

The Shadow on the Blind

Last night I walked among the lamps that gleamed,
 And saw a shadow on a window blind,
A moving shadow; and the picture seemed
 To call some scene to mind.

I looked again; a dark form to and fro
 Swayed softly as to music full of rest,
Bent low, bent lower: -- Still I did not know.
 And then, at last, I guessed.

And through the night came all old memories flocking,
 White memories like the snowflakes round me whirled.
"All's well!" I said; "The mothers still sit rocking
 The cradles of the world!"

Roderic Quinn.

The House of the Commonwealth

We sent a word across the seas that said,
 "The house is finished and the doors are wide,
  Come, enter in.
A stately house it is, with tables spread,
 Where men in liberty and love abide
  With hearts akin.

"Behold, how high our hands have lifted it!
 The soil it stands upon is pure and sweet
  As are our skies.
Our title deeds in holy sweat are writ,
 Not red accusing blood -- and 'neath our feet
  No foeman lies."

And England, Mother England, leans her face
 Upon her hand and feels her blood burn young
  At what she sees:
The image here of that fair strength and grace
 That made her feared and loved and sought and sung
  Through centuries.

What chorus shall we lift, what song of joy,

What boom of seaward cannon, roll of drums?
The majesty of nationhood demands
A burst of royal sounds, as when a victor comes
From peril of a thousand foes;
An empire's honour saved from death
Brought home again; an added rose
Of victory upon its wreath.
In this wise men have greeted kings,
In name or fame,
But such acclaim
Were vain and emptiest of things
If love were silent, drawn apart,
And mute the People's mighty heart.

The love that ivy-like an ancient land doth cherish,
It grows not in a day, nor in a year doth perish.
 But, little leaf by leaf,
It creeps along the walls and wreathes the ramparts hoary.
The sun that gives it strength -- it is a nation's glory;
 The dew, a people's grief.

The love that ivy-like around a home-land lingers,
With soft embrace of breast and green, caressive fingers,
 We are too young to know.
Not ours the glory-dome, the monuments and arches
At thought of which takes arms the blood, and proudly marches
 Exultant o'er the foe.

Green lands undesolated
For no avengement cry;
No feud of race unsated
Leaps out again to triumph,
Leaps out again to triumph, or to die!

Attendant here to-day in heart and mind
Must be all lovers of mankind,
Attendant, too, the souls sublime --
The Prophet-souls of every clime,
Who, living, in a tyrant's time,
Yet thought and wrought and sought to break
The chains about mankind and make
A man where men had made a slave:
Who all intent to lift and save
Beheld the flag of Freedom wave
And scorned the prison or the grave;
For whom the darkness failed to mar
The vision of a world afar,
The shining of the Morning Star.
Attendant here, then, they must be,
And gathering close with eyes elate
Behold the vision of a State
Where men are equal, just, and free:
A State that hath no stain upon her,
No taint to hurt her maiden honour;
A Home where love and kindness centre;
A People's House where all may enter.
And, being entered, meet no dearth
Of welcome round a common hearth;
A People's House not built of stone,
Nor wrought by hand and brain alone,
But formed and founded on the heart;
A People's House, A People's Home,
En-isled in foam and far apart;
A People's House, where all may roam
The many rooms and be at ease;
A People's House, with tower and dome;

And over all a People's Flag --
A Flag upon the breeze.

The Lotus-Flower

All the heights of the high shores gleam
  Red and gold at the sunset hour:
There comes the spell of a magic dream,
  And the Harbour seems a lotus-flower;

A blue flower tinted at dawn with gold,
  A broad flower blazing with light at noon,
A flower forever with charms to hold
  His heart, who sees it by sun or moon.

Its beauty burns like a ceaseless fire,
  And tower looks over the top of tower;
For all mute things it would seem, aspire
  To catch a glimpse of the lotus-flower.

Men meet its beauty with furrowed face,
  And straight the furrows are smoothed away;
They buy and sell in the market-place,
  And languor leadens their blood all day.

At night they look on the flower, and lo!
  The City passes with all its cares:
They dream no more in its azure glow,
  Of gold and silver and stocks and shares.

The Lotus dreams 'neath the dreaming skies,
 Its beauty touching with spell divine
The grey old town, till the old town lies
 Like one half-drunk with a magic wine.

Star-loved, it breathes at the midnight hour
 A sense of peace from its velvet mouth.
Though flowers be fair -- is there any flower
 Like this blue flower of the radiant South?

Sun-loved and lit by the moon it yields
 A challenge-glory or glow serene,
And men bethink them of jewelled shields,
 A turquoise lighting a ground of green.

Fond lovers pacing beside it see
 Not death and darkness, but life and light,
And dream no dream of the witchery
 The Lotus sheds on the silent night.

Pale watchers weary of watching stars
 That fall, and fall, and forever fall,
Tear-worn and troubled with many scars,
 They seek the Lotus and end life's thrall.

The spirit spelled by the Lotus swoons,
 Its beauty summons the artist mood;
And thus, perchance, in a thousand moons
 Its spell shall work in our waiting blood.

Then souls shall shine with an old-time grace,
 And sense be wrapped in a golden trance,
And art be crowned in the market-place

With Love and Beauty and fair Romance.

David McKee Wright.

An Old Colonist's Reverie

Dustily over the highway pipes the loud nor'-wester at morn,
Wind and the rising sun, and waving tussock and corn;
It brings to me days gone by when first in my ears it rang,
The wind is the voice of my home, and I think of the songs it sang
When, fresh from the desk and ledger, I crossed the long leagues of sea --
"The old worn world is gone and the new bright world is free."

The wide, wild pastures of old are fading and passing away,
All over the plain are the homes of the men who have come to stay --
I sigh for the good old days in the station whare again;
But the good new days are better -- I would not be heard to complain;
It is only the wind that cries with tears in its voice to me
Of the dead men low in the mould who came with me over the sea.

Some of them down in the city under the marble are laid,
Some on the bare hillside in the mound by the lone tree shade,
And some in the forest deeps of the west in their silence lie,
With the dark pine curtain above shutting out the blue of the sky.

And many have passed from my sight, whither I never shall know,
Swept away in the rushing river or caught in the mountain snow;
All the old hands are gone who came with me over the sea,
But the land that we made our own is the same bright land to me.

There are dreams in the gold of the kowhai, and when ratas are breaking
 in bloom
I can hear the rich murmur of voices in the deeps of the fern-shadowed gloom.
Old memory may bring me her treasures from the land of the blossoms of May,
But to me the hill daisies are dearer and the gorse on the river bed grey;
While the mists on the high hilltops curling, the dawn-haunted
 haze of the sea,
To my fancy are bridal veils lifting from the face of the land of the free.

The speargrass and cabbage trees yonder, the honey-belled flax in its bloom,
The dark of the bush on the sidings, the snow-crested mountains that loom
Golden and grey in the sunlight, far up in the cloud-fringed blue,
Are the threads with old memory weaving and the line of my life
 running through;
And the wind of the morning calling has ever a song for me
Of hope for the land of the dawning in the golden years to be.

Christopher John Brennan.

Romance

Of old, on her terrace at evening
...not here...in some long-gone kingdom
O, folded close to her breast!...

--our gaze dwelt wide on the blackness
(was it trees? or a shadowy passion
the pain of an old-world longing
that it sobb'd, that it swell'd, that it shrank?)
--the gloom of the forest
blurr'd soft on the skirt of the night-skies
that shut in our lonely world.

...not here...in some long-gone world...

close-lock'd in that passionate arm-clasp
no word did we utter, we stirr'd not:
the silence of Death, or of Love...
only, round and over us
that tearless infinite yearning
and the Night with her spread wings rustling
folding us with the stars.

...not here...in some long-gone kingdom
of old, on her terrace at evening
O, folded close to her heart!...

Poppies

Where the poppy-banners flow
 in and out amongst the corn,
 spotless morn
ever saw us come and go

hand in hand, as girl and boy
 warming fast to youth and maid,
 half afraid
at the hint of passionate joy

still in Summer's rose unshown:
 yet we heard nor knew a fear;
 strong and clear
summer's eager clarion blown

from the sunrise to the set:
 now our feet are far away,
 night and day,
do the old-known spots forget?

Sweet, I wonder if those hours
 breathe of us now parted thence,
 if a sense
of our love-birth thrill their flowers.

Poppies flush all tremulous --
  has our love grown into them,
    root and stem;
are the red blooms red with us?

Summer's standards are outroll'd,
  other lovers wander slow;
    I would know
if the morn is that of old.

Here our days bloom fuller yet,
  happiness is all our task;
    still I ask --
do the vanish'd days forget?

John Le Gay Brereton.

The Sea Maid

In what pearl-paven mossy cave
By what green sea
Art thou reclining, virgin of the wave,
In realms more full of splendid mystery
Than that strong northern flood whence came

The rise and fall of music in thy name --
Thy waiting name, Oithona!

The magic of the sea's own change
In depth and height,
From where the eternal order'd billows range
To unknown regions of sleep-weary night,
Fills, like a wonder-waking spell
Whispered by lips of some lone-murmuring shell,
Thy dreaming soul, Oithona.

In gladness of thy reverie
What gracious form
Will fly the errand of our love to thee,
By ways with winged messengers aswarm
Through dawn of opalescent skies,
To say the time is come and bid thee rise
And be our child, Oithona?

Home

"Where shall we dwell?" say you.
 Wandering winds reply:
"In a temple with roof of blue
 -- Under the splendid sky."

Never a nobler home
 We'll find though an age we try
Than is arched by the azure dome
 Of the all-enfolding sky.

Here we are wed, and here
 We live under God's own eye.
"Where shall we dwell," my dear?
 Under the splendid sky.

Wilfred

What of these tender feet
 That have never toddled yet?
 What dances shall they beat,
 With what red vintage wet?
In what wild way will they march or stray, by what sly paynims met?

The toil of it none may share;
 By yourself must the way be won
 Through fervid or frozen air
 Till the overland journey's done;
And I would not take, for your own dear sake, one thorn from your track,
 my son.

Go forth to your hill and dale,
 Yet take in your hand from me
 A staff when your footsteps fail,
 A weapon if need there be;
'Twill hum in your ear when the foeman's near, athirst for the victory.

In the desert of dusty death
 It will point to the hidden spring;
 Should you weary and fail for breath,

It will burgeon and branch and swing
Till you sink to sleep in its shadow deep to the sound of its murmuring.

 . . . . .

You must face the general foe --
A phantom pale and grim.
If you flinch at his glare, he'll grow
And gather your strength to him;
But your power will rise if you laugh in his eyes and away in a mist
 he'll swim.

To your freeborn soul be true --
Fling parchment in the fire;
Men's laws are null for you,
For a word of Love is higher,
And can you do aught, when He rules your thought, but follow your own desire?

You will dread no pinching dearth
In the home where you love to lie,
For your floor will be good brown earth
And your roof the open sky.
There'll be room for all at your festival when the heart-red wine runs high.

 . . . . .

Joy to you, joy and strife
And a golden East before,
And the sound of the sea of life
In your ears when you reach the shore,
And a hope that still with as good a will you may fight as you fought of yore.

Arthur H. Adams.

Bayswater, W.

About me leagues of houses lie,
Above me, grim and straight and high,
They climb; the terraces lean up
Like long grey reefs against the sky.

Packed tier on tier the people dwell;
Each narrow, hollow wall is full;
And in that hive of honeycomb,
Remote and high, I have one cell.

And when I turn into my street
I hear in murmurous retreat
A tide of noises flowing out --
The city ebbing from my feet!

And lo! two long straight walls between,
There dwells a little park serene,
Where blackened trees and railings hem
A little handkerchief of green!

Yet I can see across the roof

The sun, the stars and . . . God! For proof --
Between the twisting chimney-pots
A pointing finger, old, aloof!

The traffic that the city rends
Within my quiet haven ends
In a deep murmur, or across
My pool a gentle ripple sends.

A chime upon the silence drab
Paints music; hooting motors stab
The pleasant peace; and, far and faint,
The jangling lyric of the cab!

And when I wander, proud and free,
Through my domain, unceasingly
The endless pageant of the shops
Marches along the street with me.

About me ever blossoming
Like rich parterres the hoardings fling
An opulence of hue, and make
Within my garden endless Spring.

The droning tram-cars spitting light:
And like great bees in drunken flight
Burly and laden deep with bloom,
The 'busses lumbering home at night!

Sometimes an afternoon will fling
New meaning on each sombre thing,
And low upon the level roofs
The sultry sun lies smouldering.

Sometimes the fog -- that faery girl --
Her veil of wonder will unfurl,
And crescent gaunt and looming flat
Are sudden mysteries of pearl!

New miracles the wet streets show;
On stems of flame the gas-lamps glow.
I walk upon the wave and see
Another London drowned below!

And when night comes strange jewels strew
The winding streets I wander through:
Like pearls upon a woman's throat
The street-lamps' swerving avenue!

In every face that passes mine
Unfathomed epics I divine:
Each figure on the pavement is
A vial of untasted wine!

Through lands enchanted wandering,
To all a splendour seems to cling.
Lo! from a window-beacon high
Hope still the Night is questioning!

And so, ere sleep, I lie and mark
Romance's stealthy footsteps. Hark!
The rhythm of the horse's hoof
Bears some new drama through the dark!

So in this tall and narrow street
I lie as in Death's lone retreat

And hear, loud in the pulse of Life,
Eternity upon me beat!

Bond Street

Its glittering emptiness it brings --
This little lane of useless things.
Here peering envy arm in arm
With ennui takes her saunterings.

Here fretful boredom, to appease
The nagging of her long disease,
Comes day by day to dabble in
This foamy sea of fripperies.

The languid women driven through
Their wearied lives, and in their view,
Patient about the bakers' shops,
The languid children, two and two!

The champing horses standing still,
Whose veins with life's impatience thrill;
And -- dead beside the carriage door --
The footman, masked and immobile!

And bloated pugs -- those epicures
Of darkened boudoirs . . . and of sewers --
Lolling high on their cushioned thrones
Blink feebly on their dainty wooers!

And in the blossoming window-shows
Each month another summer glows;
They pay the price of human souls
To rear one rich and sickly rose.

And a suave carven god of jade,
By some enthralled old Asian made,
With that thin scorn still on his lips,
Waits, in a window-front displayed:

The hurrying, streaming crowds he sees.
With the same smile he watches these
As from his temple-dusk he saw
The passing of the centuries!

Ethel Turner.

A Trembling Star

"There is my little trembling star," she said.
 I looked; once more
The tender sea had put the sun to bed,
 And heaven's floor
   Was grey.

And nowhere yet in all that young night sky
 Was any star,
But one that hung above the sea. Not high,
 Nor very far
   Away.

"I watch it every night," she said, and crept
 Within my arm.
"Soft little star, I wish the angels kept
 It safe from harm
   Alway.

"I know it is afraid," she said; her eyes
 Held a sweet tear.
"They send it all alone into the skies,
 No big stars near,
   To stay.

"They push it out before the sweet, kind moon
 Lights up the sea.
They laugh because it fears the dark. `Soon, soon,
 You'll braver be,'
   They say.

"One night I climbed far up that high white tree
 Beside the beach,
And tried to stretch my hand across the sea
 And tried to reach
   The grey.

"For something made me feel my heart would break
 Unless that night
I in my hand my trembling star could take

And kiss its fright
  Away.

"There only blew a strange wind chillily,
  And clouds were swept.
The angels would not let my own star see
  That someone wept.
    I pray

"To Christ, who hears my little prayers each night,
  That He will seek
Through all His skies for that sweet, frightened light,
  And stoop His cheek
    And say

"'My angels must not send so frail a thing
  To light the West.
Lift up the little trembling star to cling
  About my breast
    Alway.'"

`Oh, if that Rainbow up there!'

Oh, if that rainbow up there,
Spanning the sky past the hill,
Slenderly, tenderly fair
Shining with colours that thrill,
Oh, if that rainbow up there,
Just for a moment could reach
Through the wet slope of the air

Here where I stand on the beach!

Here where the waves wash the strand,
Swing itself lovingly low,
Let me catch fast with one hand,
Climb its frail rigging and go.
Climb its frail rigging and go?
Where is its haven of rest?
Out in the gleam and the glow
Of the blood-red waves of the West?

Or where the isles of the dawn
Lie on an amethyst sea,
Does it drift, pale and forlorn,
Ghost of the glory I see?
Is there, ah, is there a land
Such as the Icelanders say,
Or past the West's ruddy strand
Or on the edge of the day,

Some undiscovered clime
Seen through a cloud's sudden rift,
Where all the rainbows of Time
Slowly and silently drift?
Some happy port of a sea
Never a world's sail has made,
Where till the earth shadows flee
Never a rainbow may fade.

Oh, if that rainbow up there,
Just for a moment would reach,
Through the wet slope of the air
Here where I stand on the beach.

Here where the waves wash the strand
Swing itself lovingly low,
Let me catch fast with one hand,
Climb its frail rigging and go!

Johannes Carl Andersen.

Soft, Low and Sweet

Soft, low and sweet, the blackbird wakes the day,
And clearer pipes, as rosier grows the gray
 Of the wide sky, far, far into whose deep
 The rath lark soars, and scatters down the steep
His runnel song, that skyey roundelay.

Earth with a sigh awakes; and tremors play,
 Coy in her leafy trees, and falt'ring creep
Across the daisy lawn and whisper, "Well-a-day,"
   Soft, low and sweet.

From violet-banks the scent-clouds float away
 And spread around their fragrance, as of sleep:
 From ev'ry mossy nook the blossoms peep;
From ev'ry blossom comes one little ray
That makes the world-wealth one with Spring, alway

Soft, low and sweet.

Maui Victor

Unhewn in quarry lay the Parian stone,
 Ere hands, god-guided, of Praxiteles
Might shape the Cnidian Venus. Long ungrown
 The ivory was which, chiselled, robbed of ease
 Pygmalion, sculptor-lover. Now are these,
The stone and ivory, immortal made.
 The golden apples of Hesperides
Shall never, scattered, in blown dust be laid,
 Till Time, the dragon-guard, has lived his last decade.

The Cnidian Venus, Galatea's shape,
 A wondering world beheld, as we behold, --
Here, in blest isles beyond the stormy Cape,
 Where man the new land dowers with the old,
 Are neither marble shapes nor fruits of gold,
Nor white-limbed maidens, queened enchantress-wise;
 Here, Nature's beauties no vast ruins enfold,
No glamour fills her such as 'wildering lies
Where Mediterranean waters laugh to Grecian skies.

Acropolis with figure group and frieze,
 Parthenon, Temple, concepts born divine,
Where in these Isles are wonders great as these?
 Unquarried lies the stone in teeming mine,
 Bare is the land of sanctuary and shrine;
But though frail hands no god-like record set

Great Nature's powers are lavish, and combine
In mountain dome, ice-glancing minaret,
Deep fiord, fiery fountain and lake with tree-wove carcanet.

And though the dusky race that to and fro,
 Like their own shades, pass by and leave no trace,
No age-contemning works from quick brain throw,
 They still have left what Time shall not efface, --
 The legends of an isolated race.
Not vainly Maui strove; no, not in vain
 He dared the old Mother of Death and her embrace:
That mankind might go free, he suffered pain --
And death he boldly dared, eternal life to gain.

Not death but dormancy the old womb has known,
 New love shall quicken it, new life attain:
These legends old in ivory and stone
 Shall live their recreated life again, --
 Shall wake, like Galatea, to joy and pain.
Legends and myths and wonders; what are these
 But glittering mines that long unworked have lain?
A Homer shall unlock with magic keys
Treasure for some antipodean Praxiteles!

Dora Wilcox.

In London

When I look out on London's teeming streets,
On grim grey houses, and on leaden skies,
My courage fails me, and my heart grows sick,
And I remember that fair heritage
Barter'd by me for what your London gives.
This is not Nature's city: I am kin
To whatsoever is of free and wild,
And here I pine between these narrow walls,
And London's smoke hides all the stars from me,
Light from mine eyes, and Heaven from my heart.

For in an island of those Southern seas
That lie behind me, guarded by the Cross
That looks all night from out our splendid skies,
I know a valley opening to the East.
There, hour by hour, the lazy tide creeps in
Upon the sands I shall not pace again --
Save in a dream, -- and, hour by hour, the tide
Creeps lazily out, and I behold it not,
Nor the young moon slow sinking to her rest
Behind the hills; nor yet the dead white trees
Glimmering in the starlight: they are ghosts
Of what has been, and shall be never more.

No, never more!

       Nor shall I hear again
The wind that rises at the dead of night
Suddenly, and sweeps inward from the sea,
Rustling the tussock, nor the wekas' wail
Echoing at evening from the tawny hills.
In that deserted garden that I lov'd
Day after day, my flowers drop unseen;
And as your Summer slips away in tears,
Spring wakes our lovely Lady of the Bush,
The Kowhai, and she hastes to wrap herself
All in a mantle wrought of living gold;
Then come the birds, who are her worshippers,
To hover round her; tuis swift of wing,
And bell-birds flashing sudden in the sun,
Carolling: Ah! what English nightingale,
Heard in the stillness of a summer eve,
From out the shadow of historic elms,
Sings sweeter than our Bell-bird of the Bush?
And Spring is here: now the Veronica,
Our Koromiko, whitens on the cliff,
The honey-sweet Manuka buds, and bursts
In bloom, and the divine Convolvulus,
Most fair and frail of all our forest flowers,
Stars every covert, running riotous.
O quiet valley, opening to the East,
How far from this thy peacefulness am I!
Ah me, how far! and far this stream of Life
From thy clear creek fast falling to the sea!

Yet let me not lament that these things are
In that lov'd country I shall see no more;

All that has been is mine inviolate,
Lock'd in the secret book of memory.
And though I change, my valley knows no change.
And when I look on London's teeming streets,
On grim grey houses, and on leaden skies,
When speech seems but the babble of a crowd,
And music fails me, and my lamp of life
Burns low, and Art, my mistress, turns from me, --
Then do I pass beyond the Gate of Dreams
Into my kingdom, walking unconstrained
By ways familiar under Southern skies;
Nor unaccompanied; the dear dumb things
I lov'd once, have their immortality.
There too is all fulfilment of desire:
In this the valley of my Paradise
I find again lost ideals, dreams too fair
For lasting; there I meet once more mine own
Whom Death has stolen, or Life estranged from me, --
And thither, with the coming of the dark,
Thou comest, and the night is full of stars.

Ernest Currie.

Laudabunt Alii

There are some that long for a limpid lake by a blue Italian shore,
Or a palm-grove out where the rollers break and the coral beaches roar;
There are some for the land of the Japanee, and the tea-girls' twinkling feet;
And some for the isles of the summer sea, afloat in the dancing heat;
And others are exiles all their days, midst black or white or brown,
Who yearn for the clashing of crowded ways, and the lights of London town.

But always I would wish to be where the seasons gently fall
On the Further Isle of the Outer Sea, the last little isle of all,
A fair green land of hill and plain, of rivers and water-springs,
Where the sun still follows after the rain, and ever the hours have wings,
With its bosomed valleys where men may find retreat from
  the rough world's way . . .
Where the sea-wind kisses the mountain-wind between the dark and the day.

The combers swing from the China Sea to the California Coast,
The North Atlantic takes toll and fee of the best of the Old World's boast,
And the waves run high with the tearing crash that the Cape-bound
  steamers fear --
But they're not so free as the waves that lash the rocks by Sumner pier,
And wheresoever my body be, my heart remembers still
The purple shadows upon the sea, low down from Sumner hill.

The warm winds blow through Kuringai; the cool winds from the South
Drive little clouds across the sky by Sydney harbour-mouth;
But Sydney Heads feel no such breeze as comes from nor'-west rain
And takes the pines and the blue-gum trees by hill and gorge and plain,
And whistles down from Porter's Pass, over the fields of wheat,
And brings a breath of tussock grass into a Christchurch street.

Or the East wind dropping its sea-born rain, or the South wind wild and loud
Comes up and over the waiting plain, with a banner of driving cloud;
And if dark clouds bend to the teeming earth, and the hills are dimmed with rain,
There is only to wait for a new day's birth and the hills stand out again.
For no less sure than the rising sun, and no less glad to see
Is the lifting sky when the rain is done and the wet grass rustles free.

Some day we may drop the Farewell Light, and lose the winds of home --
But where shall we win to a land so bright, however far we roam?
We shall long for the fields of Maoriland, to pass as we used to pass
Knee-deep in the seeding tussock, and the long lush English-grass.
And we may travel a weary way ere we come to a sight as grand
As the lingering flush of the sun's last ray on the peaks of Maoriland.

George Charles Whitney.

Sunset

Behind the golden western hills
The sun goes down, a founder'd bark,
Only a mighty sadness fills
　The silence of the dark.

O twilight sad with wistful eyes,
Restore in ruth again to me
The shadow of the peace that lies
　Beyond the purple sea.

The sun of my great joy goes down,
Against the paling heights afar,
Gleams out like some glad angel's crown,
　A yellow evening star;

The glory from the western hills
Falls fading, spark on spark,
Only a mighty sadness fills
　The spaces of the dark.

James Lister Cuthbertson. [reprise]

Ode to Apollo

> "Tandem venias precamur
> Nube candentes humeros amictus
> Augur Apollo."

  Lord of the golden lyre
  Fraught with the Dorian fire,
Oh! fair-haired child of Leto, come again;
  And if no longer smile
  Delphi or Delos' isle,
Come from the depth of thine Aetnean glen,
  Where in the black ravine
  Thunders the foaming green
Of waters writhing far from mortals' ken;
  Come o'er the sparkling brine,
  And bring thy train divine --
The sweet-voiced and immortal violet-crowned Nine.

  For here are richer meads,
  And here are goodlier steeds
Than ever graced the glorious land of Greece;
  Here waves the yellow corn,
  Here is the olive born --
The gray-green gracious harbinger of peace;
  Here too hath taken root
  A tree with golden fruit,
In purple clusters hangs the vine's increase,

      And all the earth doth wear
      The dry clear Attic air
That lifts the soul to liberty, and frees the heart from care.

      Or if thy wilder mood
      Incline to solitude,
   Eternal verdure girds the lonely hills,
      Through the green gloom of ferns
      Softly the sunset burns,
   Cold from the granite flow the mountain rills;
      And there are inner shrines
      Made by the slumberous pines,
   Where the rapt heart with contemplation fills,
      And from wave-stricken shores
      Deep wistful music pours
And floods the tempest-shaken forest corridors.

      Oh, give the gift of gold
      The human heart to hold
With liquid glamour of the Lesbian line;
      With Pindar's lava glow,
      With Sophocles' calm flow,
Or Aeschylean rapture airy fine;
      Or with thy music's close
      Thy last autumnal rose
Theocritus of Sicily, divine;
      O Pythian Archer strong,
      Time cannot do thee wrong,
With thee they live for ever, thy nightingales of song.

      We too are island-born;
      Oh, leave us not in scorn --
A songless people never yet was great.

We, suppliants at thy feet,
  Await thy muses sweet
Amid the laurels at thy temple gate,
  Crownless and voiceless yet,
  But on our brows is set
The dim unwritten prophecy of fate,
  To mould from out of mud
  An empire with our blood,
To wage eternal warfare with the fire and flood.

  Lord of the minstrel choir,
  Oh, grant our hearts' desire,
To sing of truth invincible in might,
  Of love surpassing death
  That fears no fiery breath,
Of ancient inborn reverence for right,
  Of that sea-woven spell
  That from Trafalgar fell
And keeps the star of duty in our sight:
  Oh, give the sacred fire,
  And our weak lips inspire
With laurels of thy song and lightnings of thy lyre.

Notes on the Poems

Wentworth, "Australasia": `Warragamba' -- a tributary of the Nepean, the upper part of the Hawkesbury River, New South Wales.

Rowe, "Soul Ferry": "Founded on a note by Tzetzes upon Lycophron, quoted in Keightley's `Mythology of Greece and Rome'." -- Author's Note.

Parkes, "The Buried Chief": Sir James Martin, born 1820, Premier and subsequently Chief Justice of New South Wales, died 4th November, 1886.

Gordon, "A Dedication": The first six stanzas of The Dedication of "Bush Ballads and Galloping Rhymes" to the author of "Holmby House" (Whyte Melville).

Gordon, "Thora's Song": First printed in `The Australasian' under the title of "Frustra".

Gordon, "The Sick Stock-rider": First appeared in `The Colonial Monthly' without the final stanza here printed, which was preserved by Mr. J. J. Shillinglaw.

Kendall, "Prefatory Sonnets": The phrase -- "tormented and awry with passion" -- also appears in Walter Pater's essay on "Aesthetic Poetry", which, according to Mr. Ferris Greenslet's monograph on Pater, was written in 1868, but first published in `Appreciations', 1889. "Leaves from Australian Forests", in which these sonnets were first printed, was published in Melbourne in 1869.

Kendall, "To a Mountain": Dedicatory verses of "Songs from the Mountains".

Kendall, "Araluen": The author's daughter, named after a town
  in the Shoalhaven District, New South Wales.

Kendall, "Hy-Brasil": Hy-Brasil, or Tir-Nan-Oge, is the fabled
  Island of the Blessed, the paradise of ancient Ireland.

Kendall, "Outre Mer": From a poem left unfinished at the author's death.
  First printed in "Poems" (1886).

Clarke, "The Song of Tigilau": "Tigilau, the son of Tui Viti";
  an attempt to paraphrase a legend of Samoa, is remarkable
  as evidence of direct intercourse between Samoa and Fiji,
  and as showing by the use of the term "Tui Viti" that a king once reigned
  over ALL Fiji. The singularly poetic and rhythmical original
  will be found in a paper contributed by Mr. Pritchard, F.A.S.I., etc.,
  to the Anthropological Society of London." -- Author's Note.

Moloney, "Melbourne": First printed in `The Australasian'
  over the signature "Australis".

Domett, "An Invitation": First printed in "Flotsam and Jetsam": reprinted,
  with alterations, as Proem to "Ranolf and Amohia", Second Edition, 1883.

Domett, "A Maori Girl's Song": "A very free paraphrase of a song
  in Sir George Grey's collection. `Ropa' is a declaration of love
  by pinching the fingers." -- Author's Note.

Stephens, "Day" & "Night": Stanzas from "Convict Once"
  [pp. 336-7, 297-9 respectively of "Poetical Works" (1902)].

Foott, "Where the Pelican Builds": "The unexplored parts of Australia
  are sometimes spoken of by the bushmen of Western Queensland
  as the home of the Pelican, a bird whose nesting-place,
  so far as the writer knows, is seldom, if ever, found." -- Author's Note.

Foott, "New Country": `Gidya' -- a Queensland and N.S.W. aboriginal word
  for a tree of the acacia species (A. homalophylla).

`Clay-Pan' -- a shallow depression of the ground on Australian plains,
  whose thin clayey surface retains water for a considerable time.

Wilson, "Fairyland": `Parson Bird' -- The Tui, or New Zealand mocking bird.
  The male has tufts of curled white feathers under the neck,
  like a clergyman's bands.

Farrell, "Australia to England": First printed, under the title of
  "Ave Imperatrix", in `The Daily Telegraph' (Sydney), on June 22, 1897,
  the day of Queen Victoria's Diamond Jubilee.

F. Adams, "Gordon's Grave": Adam Lindsay Gordon is buried
  in Brighton (Victoria) Cemetery. Above the grave is erected
  a shattered column crowned with a laurel wreath.

Evans, "A Pastoral": `Apple-tree' -- an indigenous Australian tree,
  so called from a supposed resemblance to the English apple-tree,
  but bearing no edible fruit.

O'Hara, "Flinders": `Flinders' -- Matthew Flinders first came to Australia
  with Bass and Hunter in 1795, and made several heroic voyages
  around Australian coasts.

Jephcott, "A Ballad of the last King of Thule": `Mannan' -- the ancient
  bardic name of the Isle of Man.

`Eire' -- the ancient name of Ireland.

`The Isle of Apple-trees' -- "Emhain Ablach", the Isle of Arran.
This was the land of faery to the Northern and Western Gaels.

Mackay, "The Burial of Sir John Mackenzie": `Sir John Mackenzie' --
Born 1838; for many years Minister for Lands in New Zealand. Died 1891.

Holy Hill -- Puketapu, a hill sacred to the Maoris on the Otago coast.

Lawson, "Andy's gone with Cattle": `Riders' -- timber used to hold down
the bark roofs of primitive bush houses.

Lawson, "Out Back": `Mulga' -- an aboriginal name given to various trees
of the acacia family (A. aneura).

Lawson, "The Star of Australasia": `Jackeroo' -- a "new chum",
or person recently arrived in Australia, who goes to work on a station
to gain experience.

`Push' -- a gang of larrikins, or city roughs.

Lawson, "Middleton's Rouseabout": `Rouseabout' -- a man who does
general work on a station.

Lawson, "The Vagabond": `Flax' -- a native New Zealand plant
yielding a strong fibre (Phormium tenax, N. O. Liliaceae).

`Tussock' -- a native grass, common in New Zealand (Lomandra longifolia).

R. Quinn, "The Lotus-Flower": `Harbour' -- Sydney Harbour.

Wright, "An Old Colonist's Reverie": `Whare' -- Maori name
for a hut or house.

`Kowhai' -- the Locust tree (yellow Kowhai), and the Parrot-bill
(scarlet Kowhai) -- N.Z. flowering trees.

`Rata' -- a remarkable New Zealand tree with crimson flowers
(Metrosideros robusta), which often starts from a seed
dropped in the fork of a tree, grows downward to the earth,
and, taking root there, winds itself closely round the supporting tree
and eventually destroys it.

Andersen, "Maui Victor": `Maui' -- In Polynesian mythology,
the great hero who attempted to overcome Death, which could only be done
by passing through Hine-nui-te-po (Great Woman of Night).
This Maui attempted to do while she slept. Awakened, however,
by the cry of a black fantail, she nipped Maui in two.

Wilcox, "In London": `Weka' -- Maori name for the wood-hen,
so called from its note "Weeka" (Ocydromus Australis).

`Bell-bird' -- the korimako (Anthornis Melanura).

`Koromiko' -- Veronica salicifolia.

`Manuka' -- the tea-tree (Leptospermum scoparium and L. ericoides).

Biographical Notes

The bibliographies include books of verse only.
[This information was compiled in or before 1907. -- A. L.]

Adams, Arthur H.
  Born at Lawrence, Central Otago, New Zealand, 6th June, 1872.
  Both parents colonial born; father of English, mother of Irish family.
  Educated, High School, Christchurch, Wellington College and High School,
  Dunedin; thence with Scholarship to Otago University: graduated B.A.
  Studied law; Journalist for three years; literary secretary
  to Mr. J. C. Williamson for two years. Went as war-correspondent to China
  through Boxer campaign. Visited London, 1902. Returned to Australia, 1905.
    `Maoriland, and other Verses' (Sydney, 1899).
    `The Nazarene' (London, 1902).

Adams, Francis William Lauderdale.
  Born at Malta, 27th September, 1862; son of Prof. Leith Adams.
  Educated at Shrewsbury School, England. In Australia, 1884-89.
  Died at Margate, England, by his own hand, 4th September, 1893.
    `Henry, and other Tales' (London, 1884).
    `Poetical Works' (Brisbane and London, 1887).
    `Songs of the Army of the Night' (Sydney, 1888; London, 1890, 1893, 1894).
    `The Mass of Christ' (London, 1893).
    `Tiberius, a Drama' (London, 1894).

Andersen, Johannes Carl.
  Born at Jutland, Denmark, 14th March, 1873; came to New Zealand
  with his parents, October, 1874. Educated, New Zealand public schools.

Now in Government service, Christchurch.
  'Songs Unsung' [Christchurch, n.d. (1903)].

Bathgate, Alexander.
  Born at Peebles, Scotland, 1845. Educated, local schools and Edinburgh University. Came to New Zealand, 1863. Banking for six years; Barrister and Solicitor in Dunedin, 1872 to present date.
  'Far South Fancies' [London, n.d. (1889)].
  'The Legend of the Wandering Lake' [Dunedin, n.d. (1905)].

Bayldon, Arthur Albert Dawson.
  Born at Leeds, England, 20th March, 1865, of an old North of England family. Educated at Leeds and travelled extensively in Europe. Arrived in Queensland, 1889, and since then has travelled over a good deal of Eastern Australia. Now in Sydney, writing stories, essays, etc.
  'Lays and Lyrics' (London, 1887).
  'The Sphinx, and other Poems' (Hull, 1889).
  'Poems' (Brisbane, 1897).
  'Poems', enlarged edition [Brisbane, n.d. (1898)].
  'The Western Track, and other Verses' (Sydney, 1905).

Bracken, Thomas.
  Born in Ireland, 1843. Came to Victoria, 1855. Settled in New Zealand, 1869. Engaged as storekeeper, miner and journalist. Represented Dunedin in Parliament, 1881-4. Died, 16th February, 1898.
  'The Haunted Vale, and other Poems' (Sandhurst, 1867).
  'Behind the Tomb, and other Poems' (Melbourne, 1871).
  'Flowers of the Freelands' (Melbourne, 1877).
  'Lays of the Land of the Maori and The Moa' (London, 1884).
  'Paddy Murphy's Annual' (Dunedin, 1886).
  'A Sheaf from the Sanctum' (Dunedin, 1887).
  'Musings in Maoriland' (Dunedin and Sydney, 1890).

'Lays and Lyrics' (Wellington, 1893).
'Tom Bracken's Annual' (Wellington, 1896).
'Tom Bracken's Annual', No. 2 (Dunedin, 1897).
'Not Understood, and other Poems' (Wellington, 1905, Sydney, 1906).

Brady, Edwin James.
 Born at Carcoar, N.S.W., 7th August, 1869, of Irish parents.
 Educated, public schools (N.S.W.) and Washington (D.C.), America.
 Engaged in farming and various other occupations in N.S.W.
 Editor 'Australian Workman', 1891; Editor and proprietor of 'The Grip',
 Grafton, N.S.W.; Editor of 'The Worker' (Sydney), 1905;
 now a free-lance Journalist in Sydney.
  'The Ways of Many Waters' (Sydney, 1899).
  'The Earthen Floor' (Grafton, 1902).

Brennan, Christopher John.
 Born at Sydney, 1st November, 1870, of Irish parents.
 Educated, St. Aloysius and St. Ignatius Coll., Sydney.
 Graduated M.A., Sydney University, won James King Travelling Scholarship,
 and spent some years in Europe. Now Assistant Librarian,
 Sydney Public Library.
  'XXI Poems: Towards the Source' (Sydney, 1897).

Brereton, John Le Gay.
 Born at Sydney, 2nd September, 1871; son of the late Dr. J. Le Gay Brereton.
 Educated, Sydney Grammar School; graduated B.A., Sydney University.
 Now Assistant Librarian at the same University.
  'The Song of Brotherhood, and other Verses' (London, 1896).
  'Perdita' (Sydney, 1896).
  'Sweetheart Mine' (Sydney, 1897).
  'Sea and Sky' (Sydney, 1901).
  'Oithona' (Sydney, 1902).

Browne, Thomas Alexander ("Rolf Boldrewood").
  Born in London, 6th August, 1826. Son of Captain Sylvester Browne, who came to Australia with his family in 1830. Educated, W. T. Cape's School, Sydney. Became a Squatter in Port Fairy district, Victoria, at seventeen. Police Magistrate and Gold Fields Commissioner, 1870-1895. Wrote serials for 'Town and Country Journal'; "Ups and Downs" (subsequently re-named "The Squatter's Dream", London, 1879); "Robbery under Arms" (appeared in 'Sydney Mail', 1882, published in London, 1888); since then has issued seventeen other novels. Now residing in Melbourne.
    'Old Melbourne Memories' (Melbourne, 1884, prose and verse).

Cambridge, Ada (Mrs. Cross).
  Born at St. Germains, Norfolk, England, 21st November, 1844; eldest daughter of Henry Cambridge and Thomasine, daughter of Dr. C. Emerson. Married Rev. George F. Cross, of Ely, 25th April, 1870. Arrived in Melbourne, 19th August, 1870. Commenced writing serial stories for 'Australasian', 1875; has since published a number of novels in London and given an account of her life here in "Thirty Years in Australia" (1901).
    'Hymns on the Holy Communion' (London, 1866).
    'The Manor House and other Poems' (London, 1875).
    'Unspoken Thoughts' (London, 1887).

Carmichael, Grace Jennings (Mrs. Mullis).
  Born in Gippsland, Victoria, about 1867. Spent most of her early life in the bush. Went to Melbourne, entered Children's Hospital Training School and obtained certificate, 1890. Married Mr. Francis Mullis.
  Died, 9th February, 1904, at Leyton, near London.
    'Poems' (London and Melbourne, 1895).

Castilla, Ethel.
  Born at Kyneton, Victoria, 19th June, 1861; daughter of

Frederic Ramos de Castilla, an Englishman of Spanish descent,
and May Robertson, daughter of an Edinburgh Writer to the Signet.
Has lived mostly in Melbourne and contributed frequently to `Australasian',
`Sydney Mail', etc.
  `The Australian Girl, and other Verses' (Melbourne, 1900).

Clarke, Marcus Andrew Hislop.
  Born at Kensington, London, 24th April, 1846; son of William Hislop Clarke,
  Barrister. Educated, Dr. Dyne's School, Highgate. Came to Victoria, 1864.
  Employed as a Bank clerk for a few months, then on a station for a year.
  Journalist in Melbourne, 1867-71. Appointed Secretary to Trustees,
  Melbourne Public Library, 1871; Assistant Librarian, 1875.
  Married, 1869, Marian Dunn, daughter of John Dunn, Comedian.
  Wrote "For the Term of His Natural Life" for `The Australian Journal', 1870,
  which, partly re-written, was published in London, 1874.
  Died, 2nd August, 1881.
    Verse collected and published in `The Marcus Clarke Memorial Volume',
    1884, and `The Austral Edition of Selected Works of Marcus Clarke',
    1890 (Melbourne).

Colborne-Veel, Mary Caroline (Miss).
  Born at Christchurch, N.Z.; daughter of Joseph Veel Colborne-Veel,
  M.A., Oxon., who came to New Zealand in 1857. Educated at home.
  Contributed frequently to Australian, English and other periodicals.
    `The Fairest of the Angels, and other Verse' (London, 1894).

Currie, Archibald Ernest.
  Born at Christchurch, New Zealand, 1884, of British stock.
  Educated, Christchurch High School and Canterbury College.
  Graduated M.A., University of New Zealand.

Cuthbertson, James Lister.
  Born in Scotland, 1851. Educated, Glenalmond, and Merton College, Oxford.

Graduated B.A. Arrived in Melbourne, 1874. Senior Classical Master,
Geelong Grammar School, 1875-96.
  `Barwon Ballads' (Melbourne, 1893).

Daley, Victor James.
  Born at Navan, Armagh, Ireland, 5th September, 1858;
  father Irish, mother of Scottish descent. Went to Plymouth, England,
  at fourteen, and left there in 1876 for Australia; landed in Sydney
  and shortly after went to Adelaide, where he worked as a clerk.
  Went to Melbourne and joined the Staff of `The Carlton Advertiser'.
  Tramped to Queanbeyan, N.S.W., and edited a paper there for five months.
  Came to Sydney and wrote for Australian papers, principally `The Bulletin'.
  Lived in Melbourne for a few years; then again in Sydney
  until his death from phthisis, 29th December, 1905.
  `At Dawn and Dusk' (Sydney, 1898).

Deniehy, Daniel Henry.
  Born at Sydney, 18th August, 1828, of Irish parentage. Educated,
  M. Jonson's and W. T. Cape's schools. At fifteen wrote a novelette,
  "Love at First Sight", printed in `Colonial Literary Journal', 1844.
  Went to England with his parents, studied in London and visited
  the Continent. Returned to Sydney, was articled to Nicol D. Stenhouse
  and eventually admitted -- the first native-born solicitor on the rolls.
  Married Adelaide Elizabeth Hoalls, 1855. Elected to N.S.W. Parliament,
  1856-9. Edited `Southern Cross' (Sydney) 1859-60,
  `Victorian' (Melbourne) 1862-4. Died at Bathurst, N.S.W.,
  22nd October, 1865.
  Some of his writings were collected and published in
  `The Life and Speeches of Daniel Henry Deniehy', by Miss E. A. Martin,
  Melbourne (1884).

Domett, Alfred.
  Born at Camberwell, England, 20th May, 1811. Matriculated at Cambridge,

1829, called to the Bar, 1841, left England, 1842, for New Zealand.
Was a friend of Robert Browning and inspired the latter's poem, 'Waring',
which first appeared in 'Bells and Pomegranates', No. III., 1842.
Became Colonial Secretary for Province of Munster, N.Z., 1848,
and Premier of the Colony in 1862. Wrote "Ranolf and Amohia"
in New Zealand. Returned to England, 1871. Died at Kensington,
November, 1887.
  'Poems' (London, 1833).
  'Venice, a Poem' (London, 1839).
  'Ranolf and Amohia, A South Sea Day Dream' (London, 1872,
    second edition, 2 vols., 1883).
  'Flotsam and Jetsam' (London, 1877).

Dyson, Edward George.
  Born near Ballarat, Victoria, 5th March, 1865, of English parentage.
  Educated, public schools. Worked for some time as a miner
  in Victoria and Tasmania. Now a Journalist in Melbourne.
    'Rhymes from the Mines, and other Lines' (Sydney, 1896).

Evans, George Essex.
  Born in London, 18th June, 1863; son of John Evans, Q.C., M.P.,
  of Welsh descent. Educated at Haverford West (Wales) and St. Heliers
  (Channel Islands). Came to Queensland, 1881. Farming for some time.
  Entered Queensland Government service, 1888, and is now District Registrar
  at Toowoomba. Joint Editor of 'The Antipodean', 1893, 1894, and 1897.
  Won prize for best Ode on the Inauguration of the Commonwealth.
    'The Repentance of Magdalene Despar, and other Poems' (London, 1891).
    'Won by a Skirt' (Brisbane, n.d.).
    'Loraine, and other Verses' (Melbourne, 1898).
    'The Sword of Pain' (Toowoomba, 1905).

Farrell, John.
  Born at Buenos Aires (S. America), 18th December, 1851, of Irish parents.

Came to Australia, 1852; spent his childhood and youth
in the Victorian bush. Worked as a farmer, afterwards became a brewer
in Victoria and New South Wales. Journalist from 1887,
principally on the staff of `The Daily Telegraph', Sydney,
till his death in Sydney, 9th January, 1904.
　`Ephemera: An Iliad of Albury' (Albury, 1878).
　`Two Stories' (Melbourne, 1882).
　`How He Died, and other Poems' (Sydney, 1887).
　`Australia to England' (Sydney, 1897).
　`My Sundowner, and other Poems' (Sydney, 1904).
　`How He Died, and other Poems' (Sydney, 1905).

Foott, Mary Hannay (Mrs.).
　Born at Glasgow, 26th September, 1846; daughter of James Black,
mother descended from literary family of Hannay. Arrived in Australia,
1853. Educated in Melbourne. Married Thomas Wade Foott, 1874,
and went to live at Dundoo, Queensland. After death of her husband, 1884,
was Literary Editor of `The Queenslander' for ten years.
Now a teacher at Rocklea, Queensland.
　　`Where the Pelican Builds, and other Poems' (Brisbane, 1885).
　　`Morna Lee, and other Poems' (London, 1890).

Forster, William.
　Born at Madras, 1818. Came to Australia, 1829.
　Educated, W. T. Cape's School, Sydney. Became a Squatter.
　Entered New South Wales Parliament, was Premier, 1860,
and afterwards held portfolios in various ministries.
　Appointed Agent-General and went to London, 1876.
　Returned to New South Wales and died there, 30th October, 1882.
　　`The Weirwolf: a Tragedy' (London, 1876).
　　`The Brothers: a Drama' (London, 1877).
　　`Midas' (London, 1884).

Gay, William.
  Born at Bridge of Weir, Renfrewshire, Scotland, 1865.
  Arrived in New Zealand, April, 1885. Went to Melbourne, 1888.
  Appointed Assistant Master, Scotch College, which position he held
  until his health broke down. Travelled about the colony until 1892,
  when he became much worse and was removed to Bendigo.
  Bedridden for the last two years of his life. Died at Bendigo,
  22nd December, 1897.
    `Sonnets, and other Verses' (Melbourne, 1894).
    `Sonnets' (Bendigo, 1896).
    `Christ on Olympus, and other Poems' (Bendigo, 1896).

Gilmore, Mary J. (Mrs.).
  Born near Goulburn, New South Wales, 16th August, 1865;
  father -- Donal Cameron -- a Highlander, mother a Hawkesbury native.
  Educated at public schools; became a school teacher, 1881.
  Joined the New Australia movement and went to Paraguay, 1895.
  Married William Gilmore, 1897. Returned to Australia, 1902.
  Now resident in Casterton (Victoria).

Gordon, Adam Lindsay.
  Born at Fayal, Azores Islands, 1833; son of Captain Adam Durnford Gordon
  of Worcester (England), descendant of an old Scottish family.
  Went to England, 1840; entered Cheltenham College about 1844,
  Woolwich Military Academy 1850, and afterwards Merton College, Oxford.
  Arrived at Adelaide, South Australia, November, 1853,
  and became a mounted trooper, afterwards a horse-breaker.
  Married Maggie Park, October, 1862, and lived at Mt. Gambier,
  South Australia, for two years. Elected to South Australian Parliament,
  1865; resigned November, 1866. Moved to Ballarat (Victoria),
  November, 1867, where he purchased a livery stable. Became celebrated
  as a steeplechase rider. His only child, Annie Lindsay, died in 1868,
  his business failed, and he had several falls while racing;

his claim to the Barony of Esslemont (Scotland) was defeated;
shot himself, 24th June, 1870.
   'The Feud' (Mt. Gambier, 1864).
   'Sea Spray and Smoke Drift' (Melbourne, 1867 and 1876).
   'Ashtaroth: a Dramatic Lyric' (Melbourne, 1867 and 1877).
   'Bush Ballads and Galloping Rhymes' (Melbourne, 23rd June 1870).
   'Poems' (Melbourne, 1877, 1880, 1882, 1884, 1888).

Harpur, Charles.
  Born at Windsor, New South Wales, 1817; son of a schoolmaster.
  Followed various occupations, principally farming.
  Gold Commissioner at Araluen for eight years. Married Mary Doyle, 1850.
  Died 10th June, 1868, at Eurobodalla, N.S.W.
   'Thoughts: A Series of Sonnets' (Sydney, 1845).
   'The Bushrangers, and other Poems' (Sydney, 1853).
   'A Poet's Home' (Sydney, 1862).
   'The Tower of the Dream' (Sydney, 1865).
   'Poems' (Melbourne, 1883).

Heney, Thomas William.
  Born at Sydney, November, 1862; eldest son of Thomas W. Heney,
  Editor and part proprietor of 'Monaro Mercury'. Educated at Cooma.
  Entered 'Sydney Morning Herald' office, 1878; 'Daily Telegraph',
  Sydney, 1884; 'Western Grazier', Wilcannia, 1886; 'Echo', 1889;
  'S. M. Herald', 1891, and is now Editor of the last-named Journal.
   'Fortunate Days' (Sydney, 1886).
   'In Middle Harbour, and other Verse' (London, 1890).

Holdsworth, Philip Joseph.
  Born at Balmain, near Sydney, 12th January, 1849; father English,
  mother Irish. Editor Sydney 'Athenaeum', 'Illustrated Sydney News'.
  For many years Cashier in the Treasury, Sydney; afterwards Secretary,
  Forest Department, till 1892. Died 19th January, 1902.

'Station Hunting on the Warrego, and other Poems' (Sydney, 1885).

Hyland, Inez K. (Miss).
  Born at Portland (Victoria), 1863; daughter of T. F. Hyland
  and grand-daughter of Dr. Penfold, Magill (S.A.).
  Educated at Miss Kentish's School, Castlemaine, and by Madame Marvel.
  Died at Magill (S.A.), 1892.
    'In Sunshine and in Shadow' (Melbourne, 1893).

Jephcott, Sydney Wheeler.
  Born at Colac-Colac (Victoria), 30th November, 1864,
  parents having lately immigrated from Warwickshire (England).
  Grew up in the bush and educated himself. Engaged in farming
  on the Upper Murray (Victoria).
    'The Secrets of the South' (London, 1892).

Kelly, John Liddell.
  Born near Airdrie, Scotland, 19th February, 1850. Left school at eleven,
  self-educated afterwards. Married, 1870. Emigrated to New Zealand, 1880.
  Has since worked as a Journalist. Sub-editor 'Auckland Star';
  Editor 'Auckland Observer'; Assistant Editor 'Lyttelton Times';
  now Editor 'New Zealand Times', Wellington.
    'Tahiti, the Land of Love and Beauty' (Auckland, 1885).
    'Tarawera, or the Curse of Tuhoto' (Auckland, 1887).
    'Zealandia's Jubilee' (Auckland, 1890).
    'Heather and Fern' (Wellington, 1902).

Kendall, Henry Clarence.
  Born at Kermington, near Ulladulla, N.S.W., 18th April, 1841; son of
  Basil Kendall (born in New Zealand) and Melinda M'Nally (of Irish descent).
  Brought up and educated in the bush of N.S.W. coast districts.
  At the age of thirteen went with his uncle as a cabin boy,
  and spent two years cruising in the Pacific. Returned to Sydney

and became a shop assistant for a time; then clerk of J. Lionel Michael,
Solicitor at Grafton. After the death of Michael he obtained,
through Henry Halloran, an appointment in the Government Lands Office,
Sydney. Married Charlotte, daughter of Dr. Rutter, of Sydney, 1868;
went to Melbourne, 1869, and engaged in journalistic work.
After the death of his daughter Araluen, he returned to Sydney, 1871:
went to Camden Haven in charge of Messrs. Fagan Bros.' timber-yards,
and spent seven years there. Appointed by Sir Henry Parkes
Superintendent of State Forests, 1881, and went to live
at Cundletown (N.S.W.). Died in Sydney, 1st August, 1882.
  'At Long Bay: Euroclydon' (Sydney, n.d.).
  'The Glen of the White Man's Grave' (Sydney, n.d.).
  'Poems and Songs' (Sydney, 1862).
  'The Bronze Trumpet: a Satirical Poem' (Sydney, 1866).
  'Leaves from Australian Forests' (Melbourne, 1869, 1870).
  'Songs from the Mountains' (Sydney, 1880).
  'Orara, a Tale' (Melbourne, 1881).
  'Poems' (Melbourne, 1886, 1890, 1903).

Lawson, Henry Hertzberg.
  Born near Grenfell, N.S.W., 17th June, 1867; son of Peter Hertzberg Larsen,
a Norwegian, and Louisa Albury, native of N.S.W. Worked with his father,
who was a farmer and contractor; came to Sydney at seventeen
and learned the trade of a coach-painter; commenced writing verse, 1887;
was on the staff of the Queensland 'Boomerang', 1890, travelled in N.S.W.,
West Australia and New Zealand, engaged in various occupations;
went to London, 1900. Returned to Sydney, 1903.
  'Short Stories in Prose and Verse' (Sydney, 1894).
  'In the Days when the World was Wide, and other Verses' (Sydney, 1896).
  'Verses Popular and Humorous' (Sydney, 1900).
  'Children of the Bush' (London, 1902, prose and verse).
  'When I was King, and other Verses' (Sydney, 1905).

Loughran, Edward Booth.
  Born at Glasgow, 13th December, 1850, of Irish parents.
  Educated in North of Ireland. Arrived in Australia, January, 1866.
  Public school teacher in Queensland for several years. Became a Journalist,
  and was employed on `Rockhampton Bulletin', `Brisbane Courier',
  and `Melbourne Argus'. Joined Victorian Government `Hansard' in 1879,
  and in 1893 was appointed Chief of Staff.
    `'Neath Austral Skies' (Melbourne, 1894).

Mackay, Jessie (Miss).
  Born at foot of the Southern Alps, Canterbury, New Zealand,
  15th December, 1864; father and mother Scottish Highlanders.
  Brought up on her father's station, South Canterbury.
  Educated, Christchurch Normal School. Public school teacher for four years;
  afterwards private teacher and regular contributor to `Otago Witness'
  and other journals.
    `The Spirit of the Rangatira, and other Ballads' (Melbourne, 1889).
    `The Sitter on the Rail, and other Poems' (Christchurch, 1891).

Martin, Arthur Patchett.
  Born at Woolwich, England, 18th February, 1851; eldest son of an Australian
  pioneer colonist. Educated at Melbourne. Entered Victorian Civil Service,
  1862 [sic]; helped to found and was Editor of `Melbourne Review', 1876-1882.
  Went to England, 1882. Died there, 15th February, 1902.
    `Random Rhymes' (Melbourne, 1876).
    `Lays of To-day' (Melbourne, 1878).
    `Fernshawe', sketches in prose and verse (Melbourne, 1882; London, 1885).
    `The Withered Jester, and other Verses' (London, 1895).

Michael, James Lionel.
  Born in London, 1824; eldest son of James Walter Michael, Solicitor,
  and Rose Lemon-Hart. Articled to his father and became a Solicitor;
  was a friend of Millais and others of the Pre-Raphaelite Brotherhood.

Came to Australia, 1853; practised in Sydney, and subsequently at Grafton, Clarence River, where Kendall entered his office in 1857.
Found drowned in Clarence River with a wound in his skull, 1865.
  `Songs without Music' (Sydney, 1857).
  `John Cumberland' [Sydney, n.d. (1860)].

Moloney, Patrick.
Born at Hawthorn, Victoria, 1843. Educated, St. Patrick's College, Melbourne; graduated M.B., Melbourne University, 1867.
Married Miss Quirk of Carlton (Vic.). Died at Ulverstone, Eng., September, 1904.

O'Dowd, Bernard Patrick.
Born at Beaufort, Victoria, 11th April, 1866, of Irish parents.
Educated in Victorian State schools. Graduated B.A., LL.B., Melbourne University. Admitted to the Bar. Now Assistant Librarian, Supreme Court, Melbourne.
  `Dawnward?' (Sydney, 1903), reprinted in `A Southern Garland' (Sydney, 1904).
  `The Silent Land, and other Verses' (Melbourne, 1906).

Ogilvie, William Henry.
Born near Kelso, Scotland, 21st August, 1869. Educated, Kelso High School and Fettes College, Edinburgh. Came to Australia, 1889; engaged in droving, horse-breaking and other occupations in N.S.W. bush. Returned to Scotland, 1901. Now in Iowa, U.S.A.
  `Fair Girls and Gray Horses' (Sydney, 1898, second edition, 1899).
  `Hearts of Gold' (Sydney, 1903).

O'Hara, John Bernard.
Born at Bendigo (Victoria), 29th October, 1864, of Irish parents.
Educated, Carlton College and Ormond College; graduated M.A. Melbourne University. Became Principal, South Melbourne College, 1890,

which position he still occupies.
  'Songs of the South' (London and Melbourne, 1891).
  'Songs of the South', Second series (London, 1895).
  'Lyrics of Nature' (Melbourne, 1899).
  'A Book of Sonnets' (Melbourne, 1902).

O'Reilly, Dowell Phillip.
Born at Sydney, 1865, son of Rev. Canon O'Reilly.
Educated, Sydney Grammar School; went to Sydney University
but left before completing the course. Represented Parramatta
in N.S.W. Parliament, 1894-1898. Now a Master at Sydney Grammar School.
  'A Fragment' (Sydney, 1884).
  'Australian Poems' (Sydney, 1884).
  'A Pedlar's Pack' (Sydney, 1888).

Parkes, Sir Henry.
Born at Stoneleigh, Warwickshire, England, 27th May, 1815.
Son of an English farmer. Self-educated. Learned trade of ivory-turner.
Emigrated to Australia, 1839. Elected to old Legislative Council, 1854,
and to first Parliament under responsible government, 1856.
Was several times Premier and almost continuously in N.S.W. Parliament
until his death at Annandale, near Sydney, on 27th April, 1896.
  'Stolen Moments' (Sydney, 1842).
  'Murmurs of the Stream' (Sydney, 1857).
  'Studies in Rhyme' (Sydney, 1870).
  'The Beauteous Terrorist, and other Poems' (Sydney, 1885).
  'Fragmentary Thoughts' (Sydney, 1889).
  'Sonnets, and other Verse' (London, 1895).

Paterson, Andrew Barton ("Banjo").
Born at Narrambla, near Molong (N.S.W.), 17th February, 1864;
father Scottish, mother Australian. Admitted as a solicitor
and practised in Sydney for some years. Went to South Africa

as War Correspondent, and to China as special correspondent.
Now Editor Sydney `Evening News'.
  `The Man from Snowy River, and other Verses' (Sydney, 1895, 1902).
  `Rio Grande's Last Race and other Verses' (Sydney, 1902).

Quinn, Patrick Edward.
  Born at Sydney, N.S.W., 17th March, 1862, of Irish parents.
  Educated at various Sydney schools. Journalist.
  Member of N.S.W. Legislative Assembly for six years.

Quinn, Roderic Joseph.
  Born at Sydney, 26th November, 1869 (brother of P. E. Quinn).
  Educated in Sydney; studied law; State school teacher at Milbrulong, N.S.W.
  Returned to Sydney, 1890, where he now resides.
    `The Hidden Tide' (Sydney, 1899).
    `The Circling Hearths' (Sydney, 1901).
    Both reprinted in `A Southern Garland' (Sydney, 1904).

Richardson, Robert.
  Born at Armidale, N.S.W., 7th January, 1850; son of John Richardson.
  Educated, Sydney Grammar School, graduated B.A. Sydney University.
  Journalist. Went to England and died there 4th October, 1901.
    `Willow and Wattle' (Edinburgh, 1893).

Ross, David MacDonald.
  Born at Moeraki, on Otago coast, New Zealand, 1865.
  Parents Scottish Highlanders; who, shortly after his birth,
  removed to Palmerston in the Waihemo Valley, where he attended school.
  Engaged in farming work, shearing, etc. in various parts of New Zealand.
  Entered Agricultural Department, and in 1893 was appointed Stock Inspector,
  Waikato district, which position he still holds.
    `The After Glow' [Auckland, n.d. (1904)].

Rowe, Richard P. L.
  Born at Doncaster, England, 9th March, 1828. Emigrated to Australia when young. Journalist. Returned to England, 1858, and subsequently published a number of works there. Died, 9th November, 1879.
    'Peter 'Possums' Portfolio' (Sydney, 1858, prose and verse).

Sandes, John.
  Born at Cork, Ireland, 26th February, 1863; son of Rev. S. Dickson Sandes. Family left Ireland, 1872. Educated at King's College, London, Trinity College, Stratford-on-Avon, and Magdalen College, Oxford; graduated B.A., 1885. Travelled on Continent as tutor for a year. Came to Australia, 1887. Joined staff of Melbourne 'Argus', 1888, Sydney 'Daily Telegraph', 1903.
    'Rhymes of the Times' (Melbourne, 1898).
    'Ballads of Battle' (Melbourne, 1900).

Simpson, Martha Mildred (Miss).
  Born in Co. Tyrone, Ireland, 3rd May, 1869. Came to New South Wales with her father at the age of fourteen. Entered service of Department of Public Instruction, 1886, and is now in charge of Kindergarten section, Public School, Tamworth, and Lecturer on educational matters in the same district.

Sinclair, Margaret A. (Miss).
  Born at Auckland, N.Z., of Scottish parents. Educated at home on Thames Goldfield. Now resides in Auckland.
    'The Huia's Homeland, and other Verses' (London, 1897).
    'Echoing Oars, or "Waitemata", and other Verses' (Auckland, 1903).

Sladen, Douglas Brooke Wheelton.
  Born in London, 5th February, 1856. Educated, Cheltenham and Trinity College, Oxford; graduated B.A. Emigrated to Melbourne, 1879, graduated LL.B. at University there.

Returned to England, 1884. Edited "Australian Ballads and Rhymes", "A Century of Australian Song", and "Australian Poets", 1888.
  'Frithjof and Ingebjorg' (London, 1882).
  'Australian Lyrics' (Melbourne, 1883; London, 1885).
  'A Poetry of Exiles' (Sydney, 1883; London, 1886).
  Second Series (London, 1888).
  'A Summer Christmas' (London, 1884).
  'In Cornwall and Across the Sea' (London, 1885).
  'Edward the Black Prince' (Florence, 1886; London, 1887).
  'The Spanish Armada' (London, 1888).

Stephens, James Brunton.
Born at Borrowstowness, near Edinburgh, 17th June, 1835. Educated, Edinburgh University. Travelling tutor, 1857-1860; teaching at Greenock till 1866. Arrived in Australia, April, 1866; tutor at station on Logan River, Queensland, and in Brisbane. Married Rosalie, daughter of T. W. Donaldson. Entered Colonial Secretary's Department, Brisbane, 1883, as correspondence clerk; subsequently appointed Under Secretary. Died 29th June, 1902.
  'Convict Once' (London, 1871).
  'The Godolphin Arabian' (Brisbane, 1873, 1894).
  'The Black Gin, and other Poems' (Melbourne, 1873).
  'Mute Discourse' (Brisbane, 1878).
  'Marsupial Bill' (Brisbane, 1879).
  'Miscellaneous Poems' (London and Brisbane, 1880).
  'Convict Once, and other Poems' (Melbourne, 1885, 1888).
  'Fayette, or Bush Revels' (Brisbane, 1892).
  'Poetical Works' (Sydney, 1902).

Storrie, Agnes L. (Mrs. Kettlewell).
Born near Adelaide, South Australia; now resident in Sydney.
  'Poems' (Sydney, 1899).

Turner, Ethel (Mrs. H. R. Curlewis).
  Born at Doncaster, England, 24th January, 1872. Daughter of H. Turner, of Scottish family; mother English. Arrived in Australia, 1880. Educated, Sydney High School, where she conducted a school paper. Edited `The Parthenon', and engaged in journalistic work for some years. Published "Seven Little Australians", 1894, and since then twelve other children's books.
    `Gum Leaves' [Sydney, n.d. (1900), prose and verse].

Twisleton, Henry Lea.
  Born at Winskill, near Settle, Yorkshire, England, 9th November, 1847. Arrived in New Zealand, September, 1876; since then engaged in bush work and teaching. At present teacher at Te Awaite, near Picton, N.Z.
    `Poems in the Craven Dialect', by T. Twisleton,
      with poems by H. L. Twisleton (Settle, 1876).
    `Poems' (Wellington, N.Z., 1895).

Wentworth, William Charles.
  Born at Norfolk Island, 26th October, 1793; son of D'Arcy Wentworth, a surgeon from Dublin. Educated, Greenwich, England, and Cambridge University. Returned to Australia and took foremost part in securing a Constitution for Australia. Founder of Sydney University. Went to England, 1862. Died at Wimborne, Dorset, 20th March, 1872.
    `Australasia, a Poem' (London, 1823, 1873).

Werner, Alice (Miss).
  Born at Trieste, Austria, 1859; mother English, father German. In the same year the family emigrated to New Zealand, and lived at Dunedin. Went with her father to Mexico in 1864, and then to London. Newnham College, 1878-80. Writing for `The Speaker' and other papers until 1893. Went to South Africa, studying native languages. Returned to London, 1896. Now writing stories and verse.
    `The King of the Silver City' (London).

`A Time and Times' (London, 1886).

Whitney, George Charles.
  Born at Drummoyne, near Sydney, 25th May, 1884; father Australian,
  mother English. Educated, Fort Street Public School and Sydney University.
  Graduated B.A., 1906.

Wilcox, Dora (Miss).
  Born at Christchurch, New Zealand, 1873; father an Englishman,
  mother New Zealander. Matriculated, Canterbury College.
  Teaching in New South Wales and New Zealand for some years.
  Went to Europe, and is now in London.
    `Verses from Maoriland' (London, 1905).

Wilson, Mrs. James Glenny.
  Born (Ann Adams), at Greenvale, Victoria, 11th June, 1848;
  father from North of Ireland, mother member of an Aberdeenshire family.
  Educated at home. Married, 1874, and went to New Zealand,
  and has been living at Rangitikei ever since.
    `Themes and Variations' (London, 1889).
    `A Book of Verses' (London, 1901).

Wright, David McKee.
  Born in Co. Down, Ireland, 6th August, 1869; son of Rev. W. Wright,
  author of "The Brontes in Ireland", etc. Arrived in New Zealand, 1887.
  Entered Congregational Ministry, 1898. Now stationed at Nelson, N.Z.
    `Aorangi, and other Verses' (1896).
    `Station Ballads, and other Verses' (Dunedin, 1897).
    `Wisps of Tussock' (Oamaru, 1900).
    `New Zealand Chimes' (Wellington, 1900).

www.bookjungle.com *email: sales@bookjungle.com fax: 630-214-0564 mail: Book Jungle PO Box 2226 Champaign, IL 61825*

The Codes Of Hammurabi And Moses
W. W. Davies

QTY

The discovery of the Hammurabi Code is one of the greatest achievements of archaeology, and is of paramount interest, not only to the student of the Bible, but also to all those interested in ancient history...

Religion ISBN: *1-59462-338-4* Pages:132
MSRP $12.95

The Theory of Moral Sentiments
Adam Smith

QTY

This work from 1749. contains original theories of conscience amd moral judgment and it is the foundation for systemof morals.

Philosophy ISBN: *1-59462-777-0* Pages:536
MSRP $19.95

Jessica's First Prayer
Hesba Stretton

QTY

In a screened and secluded corner of one of the many railway-bridges which span the streets of London there could be seen a few years ago, from five o'clock every morning until half past eight, a tidily set-out coffee-stall, consisting of a trestle and board, upon which stood two large tin cans, with a small fire of charcoal burning under each so as to keep the coffee boiling during the early hours of the morning when the work-people were thronging into the city on their way to their daily toil...

Childrens ISBN: *1-59462-373-2* Pages:84
MSRP $9.95

My Life and Work
Henry Ford

QTY

Henry Ford revolutionized the world with his implementation of mass production for the Model T automobile. Gain valuable business insight into his life and work with his own auto-biography... "We have only started on our development of our country we have not as yet, with all our talk of wonderful progress, done more than scratch the surface. The progress has been wonderful enough but..."

Biographies/ ISBN: *1-59462-198-5* Pages:300
MSRP $21.95

www.bookjungle.com email: sales@bookjungle.com fax: 630-214-0564 mail: Book Jungle PO Box 2226 Champaign, IL 61825

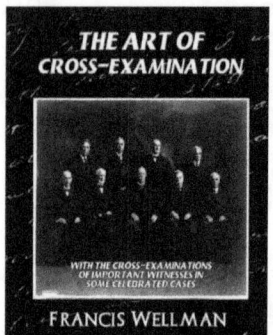

The Art of Cross-Examination
Francis Wellman

QTY

I presume it is the experience of every author, after his first book is published upon an important subject, to be almost overwhelmed with a wealth of ideas and illustrations which could readily have been included in his book, and which to his own mind, at least, seem to make a second edition inevitable. Such certainly was the case with me; and when the first edition had reached its sixth impression in five months, I rejoiced to learn that it seemed to my publishers that the book had met with a sufficiently favorable reception to justify a second and considerably enlarged edition. ..

Reference   ISBN: *1-59462-647-2*   Pages:412
                                        MSRP $19.95

On the Duty of Civil Disobedience
Henry David Thoreau

QTY

Thoreau wrote his famous essay, On the Duty of Civil Disobedience, as a protest against an unjust but popular war and the immoral but popular institution of slave-owning. He did more than write—he declined to pay his taxes, and was hauled off to gaol in consequence. Who can say how much this refusal of his hastened the end of the war and of slavery ?

Law   ISBN: *1-59462-747-9*   Pages:48
                                  MSRP $7.45

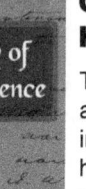

Dream Psychology Psychoanalysis for Beginners
Sigmund Freud

QTY

Sigmund Freud, born Sigismund Schlomo Freud (May 6, 1856 - September 23, 1939), was a Jewish-Austrian neurologist and psychiatrist who co-founded the psychoanalytic school of psychology. Freud is best known for his theories of the unconscious mind, especially involving the mechanism of repression; his redefinition of sexual desire as mobile and directed towards a wide variety of objects; and his therapeutic techniques, especially his understanding of transference in the therapeutic relationship and the presumed value of dreams as sources of insight into unconscious desires.

Psychology   ISBN: *1-59462-905-6*   Pages:196
                                         MSRP $15.45

The Miracle of Right Thought
Orison Swett Marden

QTY

Believe with all of your heart that you will do what you were made to do. When the mind has once formed the habit of holding cheerful, happy, prosperous pictures, it will not be easy to form the opposite habit. It does not matter how improbable or how far away this realization may see, or how dark the prospects may be, if we visualize them as best we can, as vividly as possible, hold tenaciously to them and vigorously struggle to attain them, they will gradually become actualized, realized in the life. But a desire, a longing without endeavor, a yearning abandoned or held indifferently will vanish without realization.

Self Help   ISBN: *1-59462-644-8*   Pages:360
                                        MSRP $25.45

www.bookjungle.com *email: sales@bookjungle.com fax: 630-214-0564 mail: Book Jungle PO Box 2226 Champaign, IL 61825*
QTY

☐ **The Rosicrucian Cosmo-Conception Mystic Christianity** *by Max Heindel*   ISBN: 1-59462-188-8   **$38.95**
The Rosicrucian Cosmo-conception is not dogmatic, neither does it appeal to any other authority than the reason of the student. It is: not controversial, but is: sent forth in the, hope that it may help to clear...   New Age/Religion Pages 646

☐ **Abandonment To Divine Providence** *by Jean-Pierre de Caussade*   ISBN: 1-59462-228-0   **$25.95**
"The Rev. Jean Pierre de Caussade was one of the most remarkable spiritual writers of the Society of Jesus in France in the 18th Century. His death took place at Toulouse in 1751. His works have gone through many editions and have been republished...   Inspirational/Religion Pages 400

☐ **Mental Chemistry** *by Charles Haanel*   ISBN: 1-59462-192-6   **$23.95**
Mental Chemistry allows the change of material conditions by combining and appropriately utilizing the power of the mind. Much like applied chemistry creates something new and unique out of careful combinations of chemicals the mastery of mental chemistry...   New Age Pages 354

☐ **The Letters of Robert Browning and Elizabeth Barret Barrett 1845-1846 vol II**   ISBN: 1-59462-193-4   **$35.95**
by Robert Browning and Elizabeth Barrett   Biographies Pages 596

☐ **Gleanings In Genesis (volume I)** *by Arthur W. Pink*   ISBN: 1-59462-130-6   **$27.45**
Appropriately has Genesis been termed "the seed plot of the Bible" for in it we have, in germ form, almost all of the great doctrines which are afterwards fully developed in the books of Scripture which follow...   Religion/Inspirational Pages 420

☐ **The Master Key** *by L. W. de Laurence*   ISBN: 1-59462-001-6   **$30.95**
In no branch of human knowledge has there been a more lively increase of the spirit of research during the past few years than in the study of Psychology, Concentration and Mental Discipline. The requests for authentic lessons in Thought Control, Mental Discipline and...   New Age/Business Pages 422

☐ **The Lesser Key Of Solomon Goetia** *by L. W. de Laurence*   ISBN: 1-59462-092-X   **$9.95**
This translation of the first book of the "Lernegton" which is now for the first time made accessible to students of Talismanic Magic was done, after careful collation and edition, from numerous Ancient Manuscripts in Hebrew, Latin, and French...   New Age/Occult Pages 92

☐ **Rubaiyat Of Omar Khayyam** *by Edward Fitzgerald*   ISBN: 1-59462-332-5   **$13.95**
Edward Fitzgerald, whom the world has already learned, in spite of his own efforts to remain within the shadow of anonymity, to look upon as one of the rarest poets of the century, was born at Bredfield, in Suffolk, on the 31st of March, 1809. He was the third son of John Purcell...   Music Pages 172

☐ **Ancient Law** *by Henry Maine*   ISBN: 1-59462-128-4   **$29.95**
The chief object of the following pages is to indicate some of the earliest ideas of mankind, as they are reflected in Ancient Law, and to point out the relation of those ideas to modern thought.   Religion/History Pages 452

☐ **Far-Away Stories** *by William J. Locke*   ISBN: 1-59462-129-2   **$19.45**
"Good wine needs no bush, but a collection of mixed vintages does. And this book is just such a collection. Some of the stories I do not want to remain buried for ever in the museum files of dead magazine-numbers an author's not unpardonable vanity..."   Fiction Pages 272

☐ **Life of David Crockett** *by David Crockett*   ISBN: 1-59462-250-7   **$27.45**
"Colonel David Crockett was one of the most remarkable men of the times in which he lived. Born in humble life, but gifted with a strong will, an indomitable courage, and unremitting perseverance...   Biographies/New Age Pages 424

☐ **Lip-Reading** *by Edward Nitchie*   ISBN: 1-59462-206-X   **$25.95**
Edward B. Nitchie, founder of the New York School for the Hard of Hearing, now the Nitchie School of Lip-Reading, Inc, wrote "LIP-READING Principles and Practice". The development and perfecting of this meritorious work on lip-reading was an undertaking...   How-to Pages 400

☐ **A Handbook of Suggestive Therapeutics, Applied Hypnotism, Psychic Science**   ISBN: 1-59462-214-0   **$24.95**
by Henry Munro   Health/New Age/Health/Self-help Pages 376

☐ **A Doll's House: and Two Other Plays** *by Henrik Ibsen*   ISBN: 1-59462-112-8   **$19.95**
Henrik Ibsen created this classic when in revolutionary 1848 Rome. Introducing some striking concepts in playwriting for the realist genre, this play has been studied the world over.   Fiction/Classics/Plays 308

☐ **The Light of Asia** *by sir Edwin Arnold*   ISBN: 1-59462-204-3   **$13.95**
In this poetic masterpiece, Edwin Arnold describes the life and teachings of Buddha. The man who was to become known as Buddha to the world was born as Prince Gautama of India but he rejected the worldly riches and abandoned the reigns of power when...   Religion/History/Biographies Pages 170

☐ **The Complete Works of Guy de Maupassant** *by Guy de Maupassant*   ISBN: 1-59462-157-8   **$16.95**
"For days and days, nights and nights, I had dreamed of that first kiss which was to consecrate our engagement, and I knew not on what spot I should put my lips..."   Fiction/Classics Pages 240

☐ **The Art of Cross-Examination** *by Francis L. Wellman*   ISBN: 1-59462-309-0   **$26.95**
Written by a renowned trial lawyer, Wellman imparts his experience and uses case studies to explain how to use psychology to extract desired information through questioning.   How-to/Science/Reference Pages 408

☐ **Answered or Unanswered?** *by Louisa Vaughan*   ISBN: 1-59462-248-5   **$10.95**
Miracles of Faith in China   Religion Pages 112

☐ **The Edinburgh Lectures on Mental Science (1909)** *by Thomas*   ISBN: 1-59462-008-3   **$11.95**
This book contains the substance of a course of lectures recently given by the writer in the Queen Street Hall, Edinburgh. Its purpose is to indicate the Natural Principles governing the relation between Mental Action and Material Conditions...   New Age/Psychology Pages 148

☐ **Ayesha** *by H. Rider Haggard*   ISBN: 1-59462-301-5   **$24.95**
Verily and indeed it is the unexpected that happens! Probably if there was one person upon the earth from whom the Editor of this, and of a certain previous history, did not expect to hear again...   Classics Pages 380

☐ **Ayala's Angel** *by Anthony Trollope*   ISBN: 1-59462-352-X   **$29.95**
The two girls were both pretty, but Lucy who was twenty-one who supposed to be simple and comparatively unattractive, whereas Ayala was credited, as her Bombwhat romantic name might show, with poetic charm and a taste for romance. Ayala when her father died was nineteen...   Fiction Pages 484

☐ **The American Commonwealth** *by James Bryce*   ISBN: 1-59462-286-8   **$34.45**
An interpretation of American democratic political theory. It examines political mechanics and society from the perspective of Scotsman James Bryce   Politics Pages 572

☐ **Stories of the Pilgrims** *by Margaret P. Pumphrey*   ISBN: 1-59462-116-0   **$17.95**
This book explores pilgrims religious oppression in England as well as their escape to Holland and eventual crossing to America on the Mayflower, and their early days in New England...   History Pages 268

www.bookjungle.com *email:* sales@bookjungle.com *fax:* 630-214-0564 *mail:* Book Jungle PO Box 2226 Champaign, IL 61825

QTY

The Fasting Cure *by Sinclair Upton* — ISBN: *1-59462-222-1* **$13.95**
In the Cosmopolitan Magazine for May, 1910, and in the Contemporary Review (London) for April, 1910, I published an article dealing with my experiences in fasting. I have written a great many magazine articles, but never one which attracted so much attention... *New Age/Self Help/Health Pages 164*

Hebrew Astrology *by Sepharial* — ISBN: *1-59462-308-2* **$13.45**
In these days of advanced thinking it is a matter of common observation that we have left many of the old landmarks behind and that we are now pressing forward to greater heights and to a wider horizon than that which represented the mind-content of our progenitors... *Astrology Pages 144*

Thought Vibration or The Law of Attraction in the Thought World — ISBN: *1-59462-127-6* **$12.95**
by William Walker Atkinson — *Psychology/Religion Pages 144*

Optimism *by Helen Keller* — ISBN: *1-59462-108-X* **$15.95**
Helen Keller was blind, deaf, and mute since 19 months old, yet famously learned how to overcome these handicaps, communicate with the world, and spread her lectures promoting optimism. An inspiring read for everyone... *Biographies/Inspirational Pages 84*

Sara Crewe *by Frances Burnett* — ISBN: *1-59462-360-0* **$9.45**
In the first place, Miss Minchin lived in London. Her home was a large, dull, tall one, in a large, dull square, where all the houses were alike, and all the sparrows were alike, and where all the door-knockers made the same heavy sound... *Childrens/Classic Pages 88*

The Autobiography of Benjamin Franklin *by Benjamin Franklin* — ISBN: *1-59462-135-7* **$24.95**
The Autobiography of Benjamin Franklin has probably been more extensively read than any other American historical work, and no other book of its kind has had such ups and downs of fortune. Franklin lived for many years in England, where he was agent... *Biographies/History Pages 332*

Name	
Email	
Telephone	
Address	
City, State ZIP	

☐ Credit Card   ☐ Check / Money Order

Credit Card Number	
Expiration Date	
Signature	

Please Mail to: Book Jungle
PO Box 2226
Champaign, IL 61825
or Fax to: 630-214-0564

ORDERING INFORMATION

web: www.bookjungle.com
email: sales@bookjungle.com
fax: 630-214-0564
mail: Book Jungle PO Box 2226 Champaign, IL 61825
or PayPal to sales@bookjungle.com

Please contact us for bulk discounts

DIRECT-ORDER TERMS

20% Discount if You Order Two or More Books
Free Domestic Shipping!
Accepted: Master Card, Visa, Discover, American Express

www.ingramcontent.com/pod-product-compliance
Lightning Source LLC
Chambersburg PA
CBHW081210230426
43666CB00015B/2703